NOTICE
The information in this book is [illegible] substitute for professional fitness or medical advice. As with all exercise programs, seek medical approval before you begin running and if discomfort occurs during or after exercise.

Contact David Holt at PO Box 543 Goleta CA 93116 or
E-mail holtrun@sprynet.com
First Printing on paper, September 2,002
Printing History 10 9 8 7 6 5 4 3 2 1
Best Half Marathons Paperback ISBN # 0965889769

Special thanks to the hundreds of runners with whom I've trained with from Portsmouth AC, the Yeovil Olympiads, the Ventura and the Santa Barbara running communities. Thanks to the coaches who inspired me to write this and other books, to Jeff Galloway for his quotes, and for the feedback from previous humble attempts at guiding my fellow runners.

Books printed on paper by David Holt include:
Running Dialogue, 5K to the Marathon, 280 pages ISBN # 0965889742 $17.95. An excellent first book for beginners or as an addition to your library for experienced athletes.

10K & 5K Running, Training & Racing: The Running Pyramid, 180 pages ISBN # 0965889718 $17.95. Five training phases at 20 to 100 miles per week. Low intensity 20 mile per week runners enjoy the science and running techniques as much as the 60 mile per week runners. Each level has a special section.

5K Fitness Walk at $14.95 includes extensive nutrition advice and walking to beat 18 diseases.

5K Fitness Run ISBN # 0965889750 168 pages is $14.95. Healthy beginnings to 5K races at 12 to 30 miles per week.

Best Half Marathons: Jog, Run, Train or Walk & Race the Half Marathon. 216 pages ISBN # 0965889769 $17.95. You are currently reading this the book.

Best Marathons: Jog, Run, Train or Walk & Race Fast Marathons. 344 pages ISBN # 096588970X $17.95. Five training phases total 10 to 50 weeks to your marathon. Includes extensive nutrition and injury avoidance advice.

Order these paperback books from any main street or Internet bookstore or see page 223 to order direct from the author. The bottom 4 books are also available as e-books.

Graduate from 10K training with a year at the half-marathon and lay the foundation for your marathon training.

CONTENTS **page**

Introduction

Missed 5K Fitness Run? A Harvard study showed that 24 minutes of intense aerobic activity several days per week gives you most of your cardiovascular fitness gains. But:

* You'll need to be in shape before you can do 24 minutes intensely.
* You'll need to warm up, stretch and cooldown after your 24 minutes of exercise.
* Therefore, 40 minutes per "session" will keep you fit.
* This book will take you well beyond 40 minutes:
* The goal is to run or walk the half-marathon:

Then to run the half-marathon faster.

Best half marathons will give you the tools to get into shape, or get into better shape! Some caveats:

* Start slowly if you are overweight.
* Start just as slowly if you're not overweight!
* Start even slower if you have cardiac disease. Healthy people are 10 times less likely to suffer a cardiac event during exercise than unhealthy people. Are you currently unhealthy? Start exercise slowly and only after medical clearance. Your risk will go down as you lose weight and get fitter.
* Set modest, achievable, sustainable goals.
* Hint: Aim for 10 to 15 miles per week or about three hours of exercise per week by the end of the third month. Yes, you can start that slowly to reduce your coronary risk factors.
* Which means: add only 15 minutes of exercise each week to your current exercise level.

You will still feel the difference in your fitness level in just 28 days. Why? Because you'll have done two and a half hours more exercise in the last 28 days than you did in the prior 28 days. Most of you will have decreased your calorie consumption by 200 to 500 calories per day, and be eating a more balanced diet. Net result: You're already losing weight and getting fitter.

Do this exercise for you, for how you will feel, and eventually for how you will look in the mirror. Make plans to see that healthier person in the mirror, and then exercise often enough to make it happen. Keep exercising after you've made it happen.

Be patient, enjoy every exercise session by moving slowly, without getting short of breath, for sustainable healthy exercise. Make fitness fun and you'll exercise often. Note that this authors main injury treatment advice and nutrition advice are found in *Best Marathons* or *Running Dialogue,* otherwise, this book is complete.

Some pre half-marathon training tips:

Set modest goals for this week and this month, while also looking forward to how you will feel next year, when you will have 52 weeks of exercise in the bank.

Enjoy the achievement of finishing your first mile OR your first 40 minute run.

Wear running shoes and running shorts.

Do most exercise at 60 percent of your maximum heartrate, which is about 110 to 120 per minute for most of us. After a few weeks, do some exercise at up to 80 percent of your maximum heartrate for a few minutes at a time. Later, you will exercise more intensely, and as you become more confident, run hills to develop stronger muscles. Run a variety of routes and distances and cross-train every week.

Review your goals every month.

Make your children proud of you; be a role model.

Run longer or faster as part of a graduated training program for a race, and then enter more races several times a year.

Train with other people sometimes, but jog by yourself on some days. Both have their merit.

Push yourself fairly hard for a few minutes on some days while working on running form.

However, do not hammer your workouts. Don't even workout. Instead of working out...exercise.

Be fairly consistent! Don't feel like running for 40 minutes? Slip out for a 20-minute run and stride out for 30 seconds about four times at halfway. Now that's a fun run.

Eat healthy without going to extremes. Drink low calorie liquids by the quart, not by counting how many glasses!

Once you're in shape, run a race every 3 to 4 weeks for training. It does not take all day to attend and cruise a 5K to 10K race. Most of us have a race within 15 miles of home on half of the weekends each year. Arrive an hour before the start; leave an hour after the finish and you'll have enough time to socialize. Stay for the prize giving every 4 or 5 races, but only if the race results are out fast enough. Otherwise, be content with your unofficial time. Personal records rarely come in harsh training races.

After the race, jog an easy mile, stretch, then use some periwash, handi-wipes and a towel, and put on your change of clothing to feel fresh. Most runners can be home or into their next relaxing activity by 10 am after a race that starts at eight. No rushing; it just takes a little organization.

Train wisely by adapting any program in this book to meet your needs and abilities.

Now reader, if you're not currently running, take yourself to a running shoe store and pick up some race fliers, and make a date with the next local race. Or, check the up-coming events in your local papers sport's section. See how the system works as you meet walkers and runners at all levels and intensities. Start an exercise program (page 7) to walk or run a 5K at easy pace, and move on from there.

David Holt
Santa Barbara, August 6th, 2,002

Chapter One

In the Beginning, Avoid Cardiac Arrests.

Your first race should not be a half-marathon: If you are exercising for the first time, set your cross-hairs on the 5K.

Already running a 5K once a month? Cruise to page 31 and slip yourself into whichever week of the build-up your fitness and mileage suggests would be prudent.

The first step to completing any race for over 100 million Americans is to change a sedentary body into a healthy body, a body which is fit for life. Walking for three miles on most days for several weeks should precede easy running. Gentle exercise is the key to regular exercise.

Why run: Because it's simple to do, makes you feel better, it's sociable, it's easy, it gives you pretty legs, it's great for weight loss, yet you can do it at any weight. Running gives you more energy and makes you high; it will save your life, it's dependable, it's time efficient because you can do it almost anywhere and anytime; the only equipment you need is running shoes. It teaches discipline (to run and to rest), it helps you to sleep, makes you smarter, and makes you look younger and more handsome.

Ready to run? Start with a hundred yards of slow running...then walk a hundred. Repeat several times and walk home. Gradually increase the running duration, but start each run by walking a few hundred yards. Run or walk for more time to improve endurance instead of doing it faster. However, extending your runs beyond five miles should wait until you've learned how to run economically, which reduces injury risk.

Before beginning your half marathon training on page 31, this chapter will give you:

A training schedule to walk or run your first 5K fun run.

Motivation tips follow at page 14, to keep you on track.

In case you've been in hibernation from health advice for 30 years, detailed health benefits from exercise are in Appendix IV, starting on page 210.

To run a half marathon or any race you need to:

* Deliver oxygen from the air to your heart & other muscles.
* Absorb that oxygen into your mitochondria where the combustion of energy takes place.
* Run economically so as not to waste the oxygen.
* Develop the endurance to run efficiently, mile after mile.

You can achieve all four goals by getting out of your chair and onto the trails and footpaths.

Training schedule to walk or run your first 5K.

Buy yourself some sturdy walking or running shoes, put on some old cloths, and you can start your exercise program. You don't need a treadmill. Exercise in safe areas though.

Which week of this program you start at depends upon your current health status. You're responsible for your own health. Don't kill yourself in the early weeks of exercise: this author will not pay your funeral costs. This section is adapted from Running Dialogue & www.runningbook.com.

Week One:

Not currently running? Decide on an initial goal, write it down, and set up your body to achieve it. Walk briskly for two to three miles, four to five days a week. When you're able to walk three miles in an hour, without getting severely short of breath, move to week two. Heartrate guide page 10.

Week Two:

It may take you 20 weeks to reach three miles of walking; if so, see this authors book *5K Fitness Walk*. Meantime, get into carbohydrates...by decreasing fat intake to less than 30 percent of your calories and protein to 15 percent. Consume most of your protein early in the day to increase your mental energy from catecholamines. A non-fat dairy source gives your calcium intake a boost. Later, eat big, complex carbos such as potatoes and broccoli to keep you full, with small amounts of quality protein such as fish. Half of your protein will come from plant sources like grain and beans.

Use quality whole wheat instead of breads and pasta from white flour. Whole grains give you more B-vitamins, which are essential to turn food into energy, plus a couple dozen nutrients. Aim for 6 to 11 grain servings and 5 to 9 servings of fruit and vegetables. Write it down as you eat a serving, and count your daily total. Add no fat to your food.

Fruits and vegetables at dinner will trigger the release of serotonin, a calming chemical which will help you to sleep. Smoothies are a great way to get a healthy snack, provided the ingredients are mostly non-fat. See pages 48 & 126.

Previously sedentary? Once you've made it to three miles of walking in under an hour, four times a week without aches and pains, start your interval training. After your first mile of walking, alternate 50-100 yards or 100 meters of gentle running.

No gasping for breath now. You are not sprinting for the bus. The cardiac unit staff is not following you in an ambulance! Run slowly, land gently, and then walk 100 yards. Run too fast and your exercise will be finished for this year because you'll be back on the sofa. Run walk your middle mile on three walks a week. Your fourth and additional sessions can remain walks.

Week Three:

Retired sloths can move to the next level. Walk a half-mile warmup, and then do two miles of alternating walk runs of 100 to 200 yards or meters. Do at least one of your walk runs on grass or dirt trails. Add an additional mile to one of your sessions. If you're one of the 97 million overweight Americans, write down your food and fluid intake (again) for a few days, and then find your wasted calories. (This author's book *Running Dialogue* has nutrition advice)

Exercise heartrate goal. Do your walk runs at or slightly above 60 percent of your maximum heartrate. Stay close to 60 % in your early sessions; when you've done several sessions, guarantee that your cardiopulmonary system is sufficiently stimulated by exercising at 70 %.

How do you know what your maximum heartrate is?

In your first few training weeks, subtract your age from 220. You should be able to maintain a conversation without huffing and puffing. Running pace must remain modest to allow your muscles to adapt. Run too fast and you predispose yourself to overuse injuries such as cardiac arrest and shin splints. Once you're fairly fit, use 205 minus half your age as your maximum heartrate, and see page 52.

Week Four and it's time to begin hill training.

On one of your walk runs, try several runs or brisk walks up a gentle slope. Run down a few slopes too, while practicing the art of landing softly. Run on soft surfaces.

Change one session per week to half-mile runs alternating with 220 yard or 200 meter walks. This forces you to run at a sensible pace.

Incorporate a small amount of running into your fourth walk. Start weight training too, see page 108.

Add another mile to your longest session of walk run; add it as brisk walking if you need to.

Week Five:

Add mileage. Do 3 x 4 miles and 1 x 6 miles. Practice balance. Stand tall on one leg for 30 seconds. Notice those little muscular adjustments just like when you're running. Repeat with the other leg.

Week Six:

Repeat last week, but consolidate by doing a little less walking and a little more running. Keep your breathing regular and stay positive about your ability to complete your runs…at the right intensity.

Week Seven:

You're seeing the health and fitness benefits of regular exercise, so you have two goals this week. Add a mile to two walk runs to give yourself 20 miles per week. 4, 4, 5 and 7 is ideal. Practice running for two miles at a time on two occasions this week. Do not run fast. Pace judgment is vital. Adjust your running speed to the temperature, humidity and terrain. Weight train II. During your balancing exercise, drop down into a half squat, then push up with one leg and add a few repeats each week.

Week Eight:

Take a leap of faith. After about 8 times 100 yards of gentle running in the early part of your 7 mile session, run four miles non stop at easy pace. 30-second water stops are OK. Run walk the last section. Stride a bit faster up the hills in one of your other sessions.

Week Nine:

Fully consolidated at 20 miles per week, you should be doing more running than walking by now. You have at least a 4-mile run, a series of half-mile runs, and numerous strides of 100 to 200 yards or meters. Keep everything relaxed while developing efficient running form. Your mileage decreases slightly this week, you begin resting.

Week Ten:

It is time to run a 5K, so cut your mileage to 12-15 miles. Reduce that 7-mile session to a 5. Run a continuous two miles in the middle. Ease back by walking the first and last half-mile of each session.

On race day, arrive early to register. Start your warm up with a half-mile walk and some stretching. If you've done mostly running, you can warm up with a mile of easy running, then stretch. Line up close to the back of the other entrants, and run the first half-mile slowly. Then it's time for some of you to walk 200 yards before running again.

Pace it right, and most of you will run the whole way. Each mile should take you the same amount of time. You should not slow down. Ran 11 minute miles for those 2 to 4 mile training runs, and 10-minute mile pace for those half-mile efforts? Ten to 10.5 minute miles will be about right for a 5K or 3.1 mile race.

Don't sprint at the finish of this race. If you are feeling fresh at 2 miles, pick up the pace slightly, and enjoy the thrill of a long sustained drive to the line.

Walk a half-mile or so after the race, stretch, and then re-hydrate and enjoy the day.

Training Table Abbreviations:

W3 = 3 miles of walking at up to 70 % of maximum HR

100s (3) = alternate walking with running slowly for 100 meters at no more than 80 % of max HR. Add a few 100s each session. The number in parenthesis is the total mileage for the day.

200s (4) = 200 meter runs and short walks. Follow the guidelines for the 100s.

WR(4) = alternate any combination of walking and running to reach the stated number of miles. Stay below 70 percent of max HR.

8Hills = Stride up a gentle hill for 30 to 40 seconds and ease back down. Do 8 repeats at up to 95 % of max HR, but don't get severely out of breath.

3x800 (4) = 800 meters or half a mile of running at up to 90 % of max HR, followed by 200 meters of walking.

2CR(4) = A 2 mile continuous run in the middle of a four mile walk run.

	Sat	Sun	Tues	Wed	Thurs
Or day	1	2	3	4	5
Week 1	W3	W3	W3	W2	W3
WK 2	100(3)	W3	100(3)	W3	100(3)
WK 3	200(3)	WR4	3X800(3)	W3	200(3)
WK 4	8Hills	WR5	4X800(3)	W3	200(3)
WK 5	12XHill	WR6	4X800(4)	W2	200(4)
WK 6	12XHill	WR6	5X800(4)	W2	200(4)
WK 7	16XHill	WR7	2CR(5)	W2	2CR(4)
WK 8	16XHill	4CR(7)	6X800(4)	W2	2CR(4)
WK 9	14XHill	4CR(6)	5X800(4)	W1	2CR(4)
WK 10	10XHill	2CR(5)	4X800(3)	rest	WR2

Your 5K race will be on the Saturday or Sunday. If the race is on Sunday, run/walk 2 miles on Friday. There are many more types of training to add variety.

Now all you'll need is another two years of training at the 5K and 10K, (see this author's *5K Fitness Run* or *Running Dialogue*) and you'll be ready for Chapter Three! You'll be ready to prepare for your first half-marathon.

Chapter Two

MOTIVATION

Believe that your running, walking or other exercise program will improve your physical state and your health...and it probably will.

Running too far, too fast or too often results in injury and the loss of motivation to run.

Poor planning can make you dread each up coming run. Yet, if you stretch properly and regularly, increase your mileage and quality running in a logical and gentle way, all runners can maintain their motivation to run.

Beginner runners need a reason to start. Jumping straight into a marathon training program because 20,000 runners in a major race inspired you to run a marathon is a bad idea. Half-marathon training also requires restraint.

Apart from wanting to run a long challenging race, why would you want to spend time exercising?

* You'll live longer, with better eyesight, hearing and fewer disabilities. You'll sleep better, especially if you exercise outdoors, two or more hours before bedtime and at moderate to low intensity.
* Improve your sex life as you become healthier and your feeling of self worth improves. Circulation to your sex glands improves. People who exercise regularly are almost twice as likely to have sex in each week.
* Retain mental ability longer.
* You'll be (even) more productive at work if you are physically fit. You'll take fewer sick days and will be more satisfied with your work.

See Appendix IV for more health benefits from exercise. Here are your tips on actually getting out for your exercise and staying with the program. The technical aspects mentioned in this chapter are explained later.

Make a date...to exercise.

Make regular exercise a habit, and you're more likely to stick with it. At 4 pm, you should not be thinking, "Shall I exercise this evening," because it sets you up for a refusal. Instead, think, "What exercise shall I do today." If you set say, Monday, Wednesday and Friday as your 45 minute exercise sessions, you only have to decide whether to run, walk or do 25 minutes of weight training followed by biking or elliptical training on these days. While you should do something else special for yourself on these three exercising days, Tuesday and Thursday could be your non-exercising special treats such as a movie or cooking that special meal...of 10 servings to give you healthy entrées for your freezer.

No time to exercise?

It's your life, so it's up to you how you use each of those 36 segments of 40 minutes per day. Make exercise a priority.

* Get up 40 minutes earlier;
* Organize your lunch hour better;
* Bicycle to work and back twice a week;
* Pick up the children half an hour later from child care;
* Force your child to do his or her own homework;
* Have your significant other cook dinner;
* Watch less television.

The options are endless, but your running is more likely to happen if you write down your training time-block and don't let other, less important activities intervene. Treat the run as vital and you'll do it.

Save time by training on your own.

It can take 30 minutes longer to do a 6-mile run with friends. Commutes and waiting for the second or third person, different stretching and warm up exercise wants, and the discussion about the running route burn the clock!

But do run with other people sometimes.

The commitment to run with them will help you to keep your date to run. Stretch and warm up while waiting. Add some relaxation and deep breathing exercises. Speed running feels easier with company. One famous running quote is that killer track sessions are easier in a group.

However, you should not be running killer track sessions. You need gentle sessions at 5K pace, (see pages 93 to 99) not kill the runner, and make no improvement to your 5K racing potential sessions at mile race pace. Instead of running flat out, run at appropriate pace for you, especially when training with other runners.

Most running should be slow enough to allow you to talk. If the running doesn't keep you out of therapy, chatting and laughing with friends should.

On some days, run with someone who is slower than you are. Run at their pace, but don't let them race. On another day, run with someone who is a bit faster than you are. Again, no racing, but this may be your day at tempo pace.

Extroverts should run on their own sometimes to enjoy a little solitude and actual thinking instead of mixing with other people. Introverts should join a running club and seek out fellow runners for company. You all enjoy running, so this is a great chance to talk, listen and mix with other people while feeling comfortable.

Increasing your Training?

Managing OK with 5-mile runs? Add some gentle speedwork, at a pace which you can race a 5K. It will teach you to run properly for your body. When you've been running regularly for several months, and can comfortably cover a 5K race, increase the length of one run each week to 10 miles by adding half a mile each week. This will increase your endurance.

Find running 10 miles too easy? Race some 10Ks and then incorporate 3 miles of training at 10 to 20 seconds per mile slower than your 10K race pace, plus hill repeats or hilly courses each week. Gradually increase your longest run to 15 miles, and then start Chapter Three for a half-marathon.

No enthusiasm for long runs?

Don't do them! A long run of ten miles most weeks is sufficient to enjoy 5K to 10K racing. You get over 95 percent of the health benefits from running 30 miles per week if you include a run of 10 miles. Enjoy your racing. Do a little cross training and weight training and you'll be ahead of 90 percent of the population. However, don't run a half marathon! It will hurt too much.

Want to run farther than ten miles? Enjoy the party by:

* Adding a mile to your longest run every other week.
* Hold at 15 miles for at least three months, then add a mile once a month to reach 18 miles one to two years after you began your increase.
* Run interesting routes for scenery, sounds and activity.
* Run part of it with a friend...at appropriate pace for you.
* Think about your running form each mile, especially the last few miles, but think and talk about other things too.
* Start very slowly. Run the first mile a minute slower than your average pace, then ease up to 60 to 70 percent of your maximum heartrate.
* Wander. Does fifteen miles take you 2 hours? Incorporate woods, paths and somewhat familiar areas to

ramble. But carry liquid and sugar and know where you are in that last half an hour. You need to reach your car or bus stop at 2 hours, not three hours.

* Take a bus or train out 10 miles, and run back...but not in a straight line...unless it's a huge park with grass and water stops.
* Use positive feedback to get through long runs. Telling yourself you can do something becomes a self-fulfilling prophecy...especially if you stay hydrated, and only run one mile farther than your longest run of the last month. Or you run the same distance, but only five seconds per mile faster than last month.
* Have cut-offs available. My recent favorite 14 miler is essentially out and back. However, because of the strange way that I navigate to the 5.5 mile point, to incorporate grass and trails, my direct route home would be 3.5 miles. Nine miles used to be my average run, 6 days a week, though I've yet to do a nine on this particular loop. Also, instead of turning around at the 7-mile point, I could loop round the short way home in 4.5 miles. I can also cut off a half mile at the 12-mile point if dehydration or next weeks race makes it a good idea.

Don't feel guilty about using your cut-offs. You need to avoid exhaustion. You'll also be fresher for quality running over the next few days. You can judge the right speed for you on the next long run. Don't try to catch up on this missed long run if you're in a half marathon training program. Sure the 8th run at 15 miles over a 14 week period would help...a bit. Sometimes, one less long run is better.

Spend an entire year training to race the half-marathon. While training, you can continue to race once a month at a variety of distances from 5K to 10 miles.

Remember to take a day off weekly to do something special for yourself.

Don't get greedy.

After races, take at least a day off from fast running for every mile which you raced. Running less than 40 miles per week? Take an easy day for every kilometer raced. Raced a half-marathon on 35 miles per week average? You need 21 days of mostly easy running. One gentle speed session each week would help to ease your fatigue, but don't race.

Always getting injured?

You've probably increased mileage or speed too rapidly. Cross train gently at 70 percent of max HR instead of taking out your frustration on an elliptical machine; find the cause of your injury, do the rehab exercises recommended and be patient because you will run again.

Have several goals.

Your main goal can be the big 10K race, which takes place in nine months. The goal which gets you out the door will need to be a 5K race in 2 to 3 weeks, or the 5 mile run with friends most Sunday mornings, or a quick three mile run on Tuesdays, or doing enough running to keep you in shape to do any of the previous three.

Your goals must be realistic.

Running 28 minutes for 5K after your first six months training? 27 minutes is a realistic goal in another six months. Running 28 minutes after 5 years of training? You'll need to look closely at your training to find out if something is missing. Then make the changes gradually to be able to run faster. Staying under 28 minutes could be your goal. However, running 5 seconds per mile faster may be an option. To improve you'll probably need to leave the comfort zone by running some miles a bit faster. See Chapters 3, 7 and 8.

Run at the best time of day for you.

I have a physical job, nursing. I work 3-11 pm. After sleep, breakfast and a couple hours relaxation such as reading and writing I'm ready to run. Two hours later its work, where I walk off any running fatigue. Though I find easy runs after a 7-3 shift relaxing, quality running can be a chore after being on your feet for an 8-hour work day.

Run at a different time of day.

One reason I work the evening shift is to maintain fresh legs for running. On my days off I prefer to start training at 3 or 4 pm. Rehydration and substantial eating are followed 2 hours later by a Jacuzzi.

Keep a weekly training log for inspiration.

Include the time at which you ran, the weather (if unusual), running pace, companions and place of running or route. You can include much more, but don't make it a chore.

As you age you will eventually slow down.

As your performances drop in terms of speed, your training pace should decrease too. But whatever age you are, you can still train at this years 5K pace and this years 15K pace.

Don't race all the people in each race.

You can ignore racing most runners in your age group, or only race against those in your age group. Age 42? Race against the 42 and older athletes...but take care, many of them are very experienced. Note: You'll also be surrounded by younger runners but you don't need to race them.

The 40s to 70s are the best decades of your life. You have experience or maturity: Some of you are even sensible about your training!

There are great athletes in all 5-year age groups. You can compete against some of them, or against a realistic time target. It does not matter if you are in the top 10 percent in a race, or sneak into the top 90 percent. The training must be (mostly) enjoyable by being at the right intensity for you. While it's good to do some high intensity stuff to help your racing, do something on a daily basis which is physically undemanding for yourself also.

Run for stress relief.

Run for relaxation and pleasure. Manage your life stress by dealing with it. Don't let running add to your stress. Run fewer miles or less intensely when major events happen in your life. Ten weeks at 70 percent of your usual mileage, and running fartlek sessions in the woods or striders on grass instead of track sessions is a rest phase. You can still run with friends and do a 5K race one weekend a month for the social aspect of running. Make sure that your running partner will run slowly enough to keep your runs stress free. Stressed or not, run the first mile of all runs slowly. Run the first mile of all races five seconds slower than your expected average pace for that distance.

Note: A 4-mile tempo run may be what you desire with your friend. Make sure it is the right tempo for you. Retain a small amount of fast running each week and you'll lose less fitness than with only slow miles.

Run when you're on vacation.

You have the time. There's usually something you don't want or need to do with your family. You have different places to see and experience, so see some of them on foot. You don't have to pack four pairs of running shoes. One pair will do if you plan to run every other day instead of daily. I take one pair to break in (ideal for speedwork on their third run and a long run a few days later), and one old pair for short runs, which I throw away at the end of the vacation. Take along some dead tee-shirts and your oldest socks to trash after your runs, and your suitcase will be lighter for your return home.

Run in fun places when not on vacation.

This is your hour, or more, to be yourself. Trails encourage modest paced running: Find trails with soft surfaces to reduce the impact from whacking your body back onto the planets surface hundreds of times per mile. Run with a light step upon the surface. Despite the fact that your effort level will be the same...60 to 75 percent of your maximum heartrate, you'll be running a little slower, and your injury risk is lower. When you get ready for road races, do some road running at race pace to practice pace judgment and running form.

You will often have slight aches from a prior days solid yet not too demanding session. Engross the slight soreness--the result of a sensible increase in training volume or intensity--but be careful to what degree you ache.

Unusable Excuses to stay on the sofa:

I'm too old to exercise: Start regular exercise at any age and you'll improve muscle strength and overall fitness for life. Within weeks you will also decrease your death risk from numerous diseases. You will feel younger. You can turn your aerobic fitness clock back 30 years or more.

I'm overweight: Start by walking short distances. Add distance and increase pace gradually. Walk on sand to increase the calorie burn by 60 percent, but decrease speed for your early sand sessions to avoid overtraining. Follow Chapter One's 5K program…pages 7-13.

Exercise does burn calories, but weight loss is determined by consuming fewer calories than you burn for the entire month. Enjoy your treats, but take them in moderation, or as a reward for achievements in your running such as:

* 5 runs this week, or
* Achieving 25 miles in back to back weeks, or
* Running two times one mile at 85 to 90 percent of your maximum heartrate for the first time.

Running hurts too much: Pain means you're running too fast. Warm up for ten minutes with a short walk and ease into slow running while singing a song. Singing or talking will discourage you from running faster than conversation pace. Can't talk because you are moving too fast? Stop running and walk a few hundred yards. Start running again but slower. Until you can run five miles without aching the next day, add no more than a couple of minutes or a quarter of a mile to the length of your longest run in a week. When you are ready to move beyond 5 miles, add another half mile every other week.

Muscles giving you pain signals? Don't take analgesics to shut off the pain. Ease the pace, ice and read the injury advice in *Running Dialogue* or *Best Marathons*.

Too hot or cold to run: Start with a thin layer of breathable synthetic material such as coolMax, which wicks perspiration away from your skin. On cold days, use several layers, and top them off with a windproof exercise jacket. Cover your legs too. You're over dressed if you sweat a huge amount when training. Don't wear cotton in the heat.

During cold spells, arrange to meet a friend for some runs. Warm-up indoors, then put your winter garb on and head out to lighted streets, malls or sports arenas and college tracks. Or run short loops from your house or work place if the weather has a tendency to sudden changes. Reward yourselves with cocoa and plan for that warm climate vacation spot or your summer runs.

Too lethargic: Exercise is invigorating, gives you more energy to cope with life and is an anti-depressant. You will feel better about yourself and have more confidence after running. Just take those first few steps out of the door.

Winter getting you down? Do some of your runs in daylight to increase your brain's serotonin levels, and beat the winter blues. The guy who was 15 seconds ahead of you in those 5K races last fall may not be out running this month; you will be out, and you'll run faster in the spring because you maintained fitness throughout the winter. You won't have to struggle to regain fitness or to lose excess weight in the spring if you keep running or cross training in the winter.

Too busy to run: Lace on a pair of training shoes and you can walk or run from your door. You need no other equipment or a commute to the gym. You shower once or twice a day anyway, so exercise for 30 minutes before you shower. Too busy means that you are too disorganized!

Too busy...two: When I was 13, a speaker at our school spoke about the folly of giving up something for lent. He said it is far better to commence one worthwhile thing during lent. Taking up a new activity will force you to be more organized, or you will decrease the time you spend doing something you don't need to do. Today, he would have said that we'd learn to prioritize. Need something done...give it to a busy person. Want to strengthen your mind, body and live longer...then get off your gluteal muscles and walk or bicycle or run on a regular basis.

Start with ten minutes of walking a day. Ten minutes will make a difference and soon turn into 20 minutes or more.

I have no friends who run: Running is your friend. Running is always there and is even more dependable than a dog. However, go to a track, and to several 5K races, and you'll soon find some running friends.

No one runs at my speed: A person who runs a 17 minute 5K can run with Olympic runners and with 10 minute per mile runners...for part of their runs. Potential running partner faster than you? No problem. Find out when his or her easy day is. Run with them on that day, but let them do the talking...because you will be running hard to keep up. Don't race them. Run even pace about half a step behind so they know who is setting the tempo. You can also join a running club and find people closer to your level. The Road Runner's Club of America is at www.rrca.org

I'm intimidated by faster runners: I want you to join my group...because I need someone who is slower than I am! Someone has to be the slowest. Don't run so fast that you hurt in the early sessions. Don't run more than 5 seconds per mile faster than your usual speedwork in the early sessions. The only person you need to impress is yourself. Other runners will only be impressed if you run:

* Most of your repeats at an even pace;
* Your last repeats at the same speed as your first repeats;
* Without pushing or barging through the group.

It is your race times, not your interval training times, which are likely to impress others.

When my fast guys and dolls are training at 5K pace, we can train at 2-mile effort. Or when they run half miles, we can run quarters at the same speed and get a huge rest period. We can help the fast guys by pacing the first two laps of their mile repeats, and cheer them on as the pass by on their last lap. We can also take a 10 second start and run two laps at our 5K pace while they catch us up at their 5K pace, then we can run one lap with them at our 2-mile pace as a differential.

If a group is big enough, it will split into several training levels. The person you are closest to emotionally may be two levels up or down from you in terms of speed.

Running is boring: Go find a different sport! Find new running routes and notice different things on each run. Stop for a stretch and enjoy the view. Run close to nature, and run as close to natural as the elements and the law allow.

Track or speed sessions are boring: Never repeat a speed session until three weeks after you last did it. Never repeat a speed session until three weeks after you last did it. That's not an editing mistake. Twelve times 400 meters at 5K pace is an excellent session, but the next week you should run something along the lines of 15 x 300 meters at 2 mile pace (10 to 16 seconds per mile faster than the 400s). The third week could be 6 x 600 meters at 5K pace, followed by 8 relaxed 200s just a bit faster than 2 mile pace (no more than 8 seconds per mile faster).

Do a nice fartlek session on grass with 45 to 120 second efforts at 5K pace on the fourth week and you'll be ready to repeat your three track sessions. Practice doing a mixture with your long repeats too: Repeats of 2 miles at 15K pace, 2,000 meters at 10K pace, 1,000 meters at 5K pace give variety while stimulating all of your energy systems.

It's too early to run: Not every person wants to run within fifteen minutes of waking up. Placing your running shoes by your bed, plus sufficient other gear to stay warm enough on the run makes the choice a commitment rather than a choice. Place a glass of water at the bedside and you can rehydrate before you stumble toward the bathroom. Limbering up and stretching should wake you up enough to be safe in that crucial first 400 meters. This is the most familiar 400 meters and the most likely time for you to forget to look for traffic, and damage yourself.

Early runs can be invigorating, but dress for the conditions. It should take monstrous rains or frozen water to keep you inside. If conditions are atrocious, use the time to do something you would have been doing later. You'll free up that later time for exercise.

Too late to run: Get organized. Late runs are cooler for you in summer. You'll need more clothing and reflective gear plus a small flashlight in winter. You can run two hours after a light meal, but run with safety in mind. Be seen, but run in the safest areas with little traffic; face the on-coming vehicles. Many tracks are well lit in winter. In the mid 1980s, my usual training time was 6 pm, typically at a pleasant 35 to 40 Fahrenheit. I started one memorable run at 9.30 pm, by which time the temperature was about 20 degrees. I did a favorite nine mile loop and saw only 6 vehicles. Indoor training works too of course.

Too tired from yesterdays run: You are supposed to be tired after some runs. Walking benefits runners...so walk half a mile. Running at 60 percent of maximum heartrate is better than walking...so run easy for two to five miles, then walk to finish. However, do take a day off once a week.

Too hot to run: It can be over 20 degrees cooler 10 miles away if there is a body of water, or mountains, or woods or other shaded areas away from concrete and asphalt. A forest can be worth an SPF-10 sunblock. Stripe down to the minimum, carry water, and run slower or walk.

Stay hydrated. You are more likely to consume liquid if it's cool. However, warm liquid is absorbed just as quickly according to recent studies, so warm liquids will be fine if they keep you rolling.

Or run in water: Water reduces injury risk from ground impact and you stay cool. Or use a treadmill or elliptical trainer in a room that is cool enough and has a fan. Bicycle riding sets up a greater cooling effect than running, plus you can carry more liquid. See Chapter Ten.

Speedwork feels like work: Don't feel like doing a track session? That's okay, read the Fartlek section in Chapter Three. You can do your fast running almost anywhere. Of course, you may simply need to run slower at the track!

My significant other does not like me to exercise: Provided you're a non-smoker, regular exercise is the best thing you can do to preserve a healthy life. I did hear of a runner who's wife asked him to give up running. He stopped racing, but covertly ran for an hour at lunchtime. Maybe there was no other dishonesty in the relationship, but it did not bode well for them.

If a two hour break from your partner twice a week, and a one hour break four days a week pull you away from your partner, consider taking your 8 hours of exercise preparation and exercise, plus the rest of your life away from that person. Most people work 5 to 8 times longer than they workout. We need at least one hobby which we don't share with each other. Guide and support your significant other toward their hobby.

You should overtly do some of your training so as to maximize quality time with your friends. The pre-breakfast or lunchtime easy run can free up your evening. You can also fit in a nice quality speed session in 40 minutes. Or you can get to your training spot earlier than normal, do your full session while avoiding the time wasting items, and get to your designated date spot in a timely manner.

I'm not getting any faster. Run primarily for the pleasure of a particular run, not to get faster at an arbitrary race distance like the half marathon. If you like to race, be prepared for personal records to stagnate for long periods as your body adjusts to its training. Running is a process. Take the long view, and commence a progressive training program specific to your needs. Olympic medalists in August get to the rostrum because of the background strength and endurance training the previous winter...and the prior ten years or more of training. An under trained runner can easily take 12 seconds off of his or her 5K times with a 12 week training program. It takes more than a 12-week program to achieve great races.

It really is time for a rest? You need rest every week. Most people get two days off from work. Unless you are taking running really seriously, apply the same rules to your sport. You can easily run 40 miles a week in five runs. Do a twelve once and it leaves you sevens for the other four days. Two of the sevens should include some gentle speed running, but don't make it speedwork; also, run against resistance such as hills or sand. For the half marathon, your 40 miles will probably be a 16 and three sessions of 8 miles.

Take a 25 percent mileage drop one week in four to stay fresh and motivated. Take an easy month once a year while you learn to ski, or trail walk or take a biking vacation. Run once or twice a week that month and you will maintain 75 percent of your running fitness. Also, if your different activity is as physical as those three examples, prepare for them with several weeks of specific exercises. Ease back into your running when you return.

Enter a 5K race. Place the race details on your refrigerator or a less cluttered but frequently observed spot. It may decrease your ice cream binges too, though it's less effective than not buying ice cream in the first place! Tell people you are running the 5K in 2 months, and then you will have to do some training for it.

Don't want to exercise while on vacation:

Don't do the same old exercise when on vacation, but do some exercise. See the area you're purported to be visiting by running the parks or trails. Consult a map, the locals and carry safety gear such as water and a windproof jacket. Longest run each week a 12 at 8-minute miles? Aim for 9 or 10 miles at 8.15 pace to save your legs for the museums.

To avoid having to take off the weight on your return, moderate your consumption of calorie containing liquids. Eat mostly healthy foods in modest quantities too, while sampling the local delights.

Be time efficient with speed running:

Most of this books speed sessions have you run 10 percent of your weekly mileage in one session, giving you 8 to 10 miles with a warmup and cooldown. But you can get a quality work-bout in 30 to 40 minutes.

Do five minutes of easy running, then gradually increase pace toward 15K speed for 2 to 3 minutes a few times. After 20 minutes you'll be completely warmed up, so put in a few surges of 2 minutes at 5K pace, then cooldown.

Before moving onto Chapter Three for the Half Marathon, follow a 5K or 10K training program such as the ones found in *Running Dialogue*, *5K Fitness Run*, or *10K & 5K Running, Training & Racing*. When you've been consistently running 20 miles or more per week for three months, you'll be ready for Chapter Three.

Chapter Three

Half-marathon Step One

DISTANCE & STRENGTH: MILEAGE & HILL TRAINING.

The best way to prepare yourself for the half-marathon is to spend 2 to 3 years training and racing at 5K to 10 miles. You can then safely embark on the training for your first half-marathon with only modest injury risk.

As mentioned elsewhere, this authors books *10K & 5K Running, Training & Racing* and *5K Fitness Run,* show runners how to prepare for the shorter distances. This Chapter will gently take you to your first half-marathon.

According to Chapter Six of *10K & 5K Running,* "Runners who have done 8-10 fifteen mile runs, plus hills, threshold and VO2 maximum pace running should be in shape to race a decent half-marathon. If your weekly mileage is over 50, an eighteen mile run at 9, 6 and 3 weeks prior to the Half-marathon will improve your ability to process fats for energy and perhaps increase your aerobic capacity and leg strength. It may improve your half-marathon time; it should at least make the distance feel more manageable."

Ten K Running then suggested its readers take a look at this authors three web pages on half-marathon training.

Here is an expanded look at preparation for racing at the half-marathon. With any luck, these schedules will keep you away from the marathon for several years.

The 20 miles per week recreational runner should restrain him or herself to 5K races and to running an occasional 10K. They lack sufficient training to race a half-marathon.

If you want to enjoy the event, half-marathon running requires a commitment to more mileage. Recreational runners could use a 30 mile per week training schedule for 6 months to prepare for a half-marathon. However, they should probably move up to a more realistic 40 miles per week schedule. They'll be better off if they spend an entire year of training for the half-marathon at 40 miles per week.

Modestly high mileage with long runs plus hills set you up for all long distance racing by building an aerobic and strength base. Long runs and hills improve your leg muscle strength and running economy, helping you to use less oxygen per mile and decrease injury risk. Aerobic capacity and strength are essential to completing, let alone racing all distances--the Long Run is vital for the half-marathon.

How far should a half-marathon runner go in a long run?

Renowned New Zealand coach Arthur Lydiard felt that all distance runners should run as far as their bodies are able to, just like a marathon runner does. Racing a half-marathon is unlikely to be successful on low mileage. While some talented 30-mile per week runners will run faster half-marathons than less gifted 50-mile per week runners, most people will run faster on more mileage. You need to build a sound aerobic base for all distance racing, especially for racing at 13.1 miles.

The more miles you are able to physically put in, (as opposed to those miles which you'd like to think you did), the stronger your legs will be, and you will race faster. Low mileage training is great for recreation, but there is only one reason why a half-marathon runner should be doing less mileage than a marathon runner. The reason is temporary: that he or she is in a steady build-up.

As this author stated in 10K & 5K Running, even at the 10K, you need a 15 mile distance run most weeks to build stamina, aerobic pathways, mitochondria, red blood cells, and to prepare you for the aerobic strides and fartlek, threshold pace training, and VO2 max enhancing intervals which will be discussed in Chapter Seven and Eight.

According to two-time Olympian and author Jeff Galloway, "The long run is the most important component in your training program, and bestows more conditioning benefit than any other."

Long distance runs stimulate Red Blood Cells (RBCs) production, increase the number and size of your Mitochondria, and the amount of glycogen (a source of sugar) stored in your muscles. You will transport more oxygen to your muscles, and you'll be able to use more of that oxygen to produce energy from the copious sugar supply.

Muscles use the chemical compound ATP (adenosine triphosphate) as their energy source to power their contractions. Even well conditioned muscles store very little ATP, so it must be re-synthesized at the same rate at which it is used. Long runs stimulate your aerobic endurance to bring in the nutrients required to re-process ATP.

* Run long and often to increase your VO2 maximum...the maximum amount of oxygen which you can absorb in a given time.
* Run long and often to increase your hearts contractile force to send blood to your muscles with that oxygen.
* Run long and often to stimulate your red blood cells which actually carry the oxygen to your muscles.

You can produce some ATP without oxygen, using the anaerobic pathways. The problem with the anaerobic system is that it produces the waste product, lactic acid, which eventually decreases your muscle cells ability to work efficiently. Aerobic energy pathways are much more efficient than anaerobic pathways.

Long runs at 60-70 percent of maximum heartrate also teach your muscles to burn fat as fuel. Burning fat takes 10 percent more oxygen per mile than burning glycogen or sugar; fat burning predominates only at modest speeds. The last few miles of your longest runs are the miles which bring you the most benefit regarding fat use efficiency. Run 18 miles once every three weeks for 6-12 months during your half-marathon preparation, and you're well on the way to educating your muscle cells in the art of fat use.

Fast running predominantly burns carbohydrates. Run a sensible speed session the day before your long run and you'll deplete your glycogen reserves somewhat. You will then get a still greater fat use education lesson the next day during your long run.

Start your runs at 60 percent of max HR, and you'll burn more fat early in the run. Speed up to 70 percent of max HR for the second half of the run, and you'll be able to burn the glycogen supply which you had conserved. This practice is still more effective if you are on high mileage.

How do you know what your maximum heartrate is?

Newer runners can subtract their age from 220. Or calculate your maximum by starting from your resting HR, as described on page 53. When you've run your first half-marathon, you'll be ready for the maximum heartrate test as described on pages 53 to 54.

Running at 60 to 70 percent of your maximum HR will allow you talk easily in 8 to 10 word sentences. You should not be huffing and puffing 2 to 3 word responses...that comes in Chapter Seven.

If you're running 45 miles per week, your regular 18 miler would be 40 percent of your weekly miles. Forty percent in one run is a daunting task, unless you restrict your speed. Perfect, because you now have an excuse to run slowly. The ideal training speed is not much faster than a jog, or sixty percent of your maximum heartrate.

Two weeks out of every three, you'll only run 15 miles. A fifteen-mile run is only one-third of your mileage, and it leaves you 30 miles to stretch among the other six days. Your second longest run should be a 10. Your two main speed sessions...one of hills and one of fartlek for at least the first 10 weeks, will need to be three to four miles at pace, plus two miles each side as warm-up and cooldown.

Your typical half-marathon training week is therefore:

Day One: 8 times 600-meter hill repeats, add your warmup and cooldown to total 7 miles.

Day Two: Steady run at up to 70 percent max heartrate for 15 miles.

Day Four: Fartlek training for 3 to 4 miles worth at 15K to 5K race pace. The session will total 8 miles.

Day six: Second longest run...a 10 miler.

Which leaves you five miles on one of your three easy days. 40 mile per week runners give the five miler a miss.

This schedule is excellent for the majority of runners who desire plenty of rest days and time to cope with busy lives.

Competitive runners would think this was a minimalist training system. If you are an experienced runner, and would like to get closer to your potential, you'll need to build toward a six to eight mile run on most easy or rest days. Do these easy runs slowly enough and they will give you recovery from the fast training, yet they also set you up for the fast training. They add to your muscle strength and endurance base. Meantime, cross train on easy days.

More important than those six to eight mile runs though is the second long run. It is the second most important session of the week. The second longest run should be 75 percent of your longest run. Run a 15 each Sunday? Do an 11 midweek. Weekend run 18? It's a 12 or 13 midweek. This medium length run adds to your aerobic endurance, the most important ability you need for half-marathon racing. When you've got used to your new and higher mileage, run half of this midweek run at close to 80 percent of your max heartrate to set yourself up for Chapter Seven's training.

Hill Repeats

If you are going to race well at the half-marathon, you need more than Long Runs and decent mileage.

You'll also need hill training, or some other form of resistance training for strength and to maintain knee lift during your mileage build-up. Lydiard said the best form of resistance training for leg muscle strength is hill repeats. Hills improve your strength endurance and improve your ability to maintain quality muscle contractions during the entire half-marathon. Strength from forceful hill training decreases the number of muscle cells you to use to maintain race pace. Keep your hill repeats at 5K to 10K intensity.

Some coaches say you don't need as much knee lift for the half-marathon as you do for the 10K; most agree that high knees are inefficient at long distances. However, this is training, so while doing hill repeats, "pick up those knees," as the passer-by insult goes. In races, keep the knees low.

More of your hill repeat sessions can be long repeats at close to 10K effort to work on endurance at modest pace, instead of short hills at 2-mile intensity. Practice running your hills with a high knee lift because it's the best way to build strength in your upper leg muscles and calves.

Run some downhills on a soft surface to practice running form and to work the soleus, hamstring and butt muscles. The downhill strides are for relaxing and lengthening your stride, or for increasing leg speed: they are not for sprinting at maximum speed. Develop a fast running style with these downhills by running 5K to 10K pace while at 15K effort.

Do some bounding or other plyometrics to enhance your strength; you don't need a huge volume of bounding. Jump higher in the air with high knees for 10-12 times 30 seconds twice a week on a soft surface such as a sandy beach or grass. Bound up high and also go for distance on each stride to improve push-off and knee lift. Bounding, skipping, hopping and hill reps will decrease the tendency for calf cramps because your calf muscles will be well conditioned.

Jumping can also improve your running economy by 4 percent. After a warm up, stand with your feet together. Bend your knees, then jump up as high as possible and land with slightly bent knees. After a few weeks, graduate to single leg jumps. Take a few seconds between each jump. Start with only 5 and build up to 15 on three days a week. Also, to emphasize the calf, try a more continuous exercise. With feet together, spring up into the air 6 inches or so for 10 jumps, three times per week. Build up to 30 efforts. The goal is not to make your leg muscles sore in your early sessions. Add a few reps each week using the overload concept and keep injury risk from achy muscles low.

Another way to improve your hip flexors and hence your knee lift is with knee raises. Hang from a bar and lift one knee as high as possible. Repeat 15 to 20 times per leg.

During your weight training starting at page 108, include free-weight exercises in which you're also weight bearing. You work several muscle groups at the same time and improve balance and coordination. Half squats and lunges work well, yet the simplest is step-ups, which you can easily do outside, and about 5 minutes into your run.

Back to hills. Run about 5 percent of your weekly miles as hill repeats, or through deep sand or mud.

You could run your hills in a less formal way by surging the hills on a hilly loop. However, timing repeats will help you to see how you are progressing. Adding extra reps is easier too. It's difficult to rationalize repeating two or three hills on a 6-mile hilly loop. Man's inclination is to be satisfied with one loop and no extras. You're more likely to do your extra reps if you move steadily from 6 toward 12 hill repeats over a 3-month period. Be sure to run them at 5K intensity, not mile pace intensity. Five K intensity gives you an appetite for more repeats. Mile intensity leaves many runners dreading hill sessions, and then avoiding hill work because they've made it seem like work.

The best use of a hilly course is to:

* Prepare yourself for the rigors of hill training; including
* Preparing your calf muscles and Achilles tendons for hill reps (do stretch them regularly);
* Then: run hilly loops in addition to hill reps;
* Avoid using hilly loops as a substitute for hill repeats.

Sometimes your non-running stresses require that you do a more relaxed session instead of hill repeats. Cruising (but not charging) up the hills at 5K intensity, while running the rest of the course at steady pace, can be a pleasant substitute for hill repeats once every three to four weeks.

Hills and other resistance training add mental and physical toughness. Hills within a race should not cause you problems because you will have run similar hills faster in training. Aim to reach 90-95 percent of your maximum heartrate by the top of each hill repeat. Run a few short efforts at 2-mile race pace when practicing downhill strides, and hilly half-marathon courses will not intimidate you.

The Second Speed Session.

Fartlek (Swedish for speedplay) is the most relaxing way to run your other speed session during step one of your training. Fartlek gives you recovery from the strength training you do during hill repeats, in the gym, and on your long runs. You can play at 5K to 15K race pace, and in efforts of 200 to 1,600 meters. Run about 10 percent of your weekly miles in one fartlek session.

As Olympian Jeff Galloway says, "Fartlek is the best form of speed training, because it conditions the mind for racing, as it gears up the body for top performance." If you're running 60 miles per week...build gently to 6 miles at speed during the fartlek session.

The easy running between fast efforts, plus the warm-up and cooldown gives you 10 to 11 miles of running for this session. High mileage runners will thus have three or four runs of 10 miles or more each week.

Stay relaxed during fartlek sessions and this faster than half-marathon pace running gives a tremendous training effect. If you're new to quality running, add a half-mile of fartlek as short easy strides every other week until you reach 10 percent of your weekly miles. Gradually convert to longer efforts as you get used to the quantity, and as your muscles gain the strength benefit from your long runs and hill sessions. Then increase speed from 15K to 10K pace for some of the long efforts. Chapters 7 and 8 show why 15K and 5K paces are the ideal training speeds for fartlek.

Use the day four fartlek in the up-coming schedule to work on a good economical running form; run on soft surfaces and trails when possible. Practice the art of running downhill for a few of your efforts.

Speed running helps your running form…if you think about your form. So, keep your head upright to help your breathing, relax your shoulders instead of being hunched up and rigid. Run tall and upright to inflate your lungs and extend your stride. Elbows at 90 degrees and move your arms back and forward, not across your chest. Keep your hands loose, as if you're holding onto a pigeons egg. Tuck those hips under your torso. Use short rapid strides as if landing onto hot coals. Land on the outside of your foot and roll rapidly forward to push off from your toes.

Eventually, you'll alternate mainly short efforts of fartlek running at close to 5K pace with long efforts at 15K pace. The numbers 16 / 2.0 in this schedule ask you to run 16 efforts of between 100 and 300 meters to get a total of 2.0 miles at speed. You could cruise 5 x 300 meters, then 8 x 200 at a track, but keep the recovery short so that you only run at 5K pace. Faster than 5K pace is counter-productive.

Run the long fartlek efforts at half-marathon to 15K race pace. 6 / 3.5 means six efforts of 800 to 1,600 meters to get a total 3.5 miles. Two times 1,200 meters, then 4 x 800 meters achieves the same goal. Do restrict your pace.

In this schedule, you achieve your maximum of 4 miles of short efforts in week 12 and 5 miles of long efforts in week 17. This lets you focus on the final increase of hill reps and the long run during the last phase of your build-up.

10K races are just as good as the 12K and 10-mile race if a 10K is more convenient to your location. You get to run a bit faster of course, or you can run a six-mile warmup to get a feel for the fatigue you would experience at the end of a 10-mile race. Reconnoiter the joys of the half-marathon at week 29 (or week 33 if you repeated one months training).

How Long should you stay in Step One?

Had a year at 10K racing? Run a 15 miler most weeks? Run 4 to 6 miles of speedwork twice a week for a year?

You can run a sixteen and a seventeen first, or go straight to an eighteen for your long run. Decrease your speed session by one mile during the week of your first eighteen. Run three fairly hard weeks, then take an easier week to consolidate your increased training...and to race at 5K to 10 miles. After your sixth 18 mile run, do your first half-marathon and cruise to Step Two on page 83.

Coming from a lower mileage background?

Aim for a gradual increase in training quantity, while also adding small amounts of quality running. Overall, your training load needs to rise progressively over several months. The overload training principle requires that you apply a modest stress to your muscles, give them time and some rest and they'll get stronger.

Add just five miles per month to your weekly training and you'll be running 30 miles per week more by month six! You can go from 20 miles to 50 per week in 6 months. Your half-marathon race times will improve for another six months at this increased training level. It takes months to reap the running endurance and leg strength gains.

Note: Days One and Two of the up-coming program will typically be Saturday and Sunday. Days Four and Six will usually be Tuesday and Thursday to spread your training load. You can cross train or run easy on two other days. Cross training details are on pages 108 to 147.
If you start this program as a 20 miles per week recreational runner, your weekly training will progress like this:

	Day One Hill reps (in meters)	*Two* Long run	*Four* Fartlek	*Six* Medium run	Total miles
Wk One	4 x 400	5 miles	12 / 1.5	4	19.5
Two	3 x 600	6	3 / 2.0	5	22.5
Three	6 x 200	7	16 / 2.0	6	24
Four	3 x 300	7	3 / 2.0	5	22

Every 4th or 5th week is easy to rest up for a race. On day one, run the 300-meter reps on flat grass at 5K pace. You should not run a heavy session of hills in the 7 days before any race. You might like to run the fartlek session on day one, and run the shorter session of 300s 4 days pre-race on day four. The 15 to 20 mile per week recreational runner increases mileage to an average of only 22, but:

* Learns to run hills slowly enough to avoid exhaustion.
* Learns the art and pace of speedplay to improve running form. Homo Erectus got its name from being more upright

than its predecessors. Efficient running form requires good posture. Your head weighs 10 to 12 pounds so keep it still and directly above your shoulders; keep your shoulders directly above your hips and everything nicely aligned when your feet touch the ground on each stride.

* Learns to take short, yet rapid strides during all running, to reduce injury risk. By landing midfoot and rolling rapidly through the ankles for quick cadence, you can stay low to the ground, lowering landing shock. Run over the ground with a light step instead of through the ground. Practice short strides at 90 to 95 per minute for each foot per minute during easy runs *and* speed running, and you'll run more economically.

* Increases the long run by a magnificent 40 percent to 7 miles. Note: Had you increased mileage by the maximum recommended 10 percent per week, you could be at 29 miles...close to the average for weeks 5 to 8. However, you have added fast running, so don't rush to higher mileage. Instead, learn to run fast and efficiently while gradually increasing mileage.

Here's how to make gentle progression.

Wk #	Hills	V. Long	Fartlek	Long	Total
Five	Race 5K	7 miles	20 / 2.5	6	26.5
Six	6 x 400	8 miles	5 / 3.0	7	27.5
Seven	4 x 600	9	24 / 3.0	7	28.5
8	10 x 200	10	6 / 3.5	8	31
9	5 x 300	8	20 / 2.5	7	26
10	Race 8K	9	28 / 3.5	8	35.5
11	8 x 400	11	6 / 4.0	9	34
12	6 x 600	12	28 / 4.0	9	35
13	16 x 200	13	6 / 4.0	9	36
14	8 x 300	10	20 / 2.5	7	29

You can stay at 35 miles per week if you wish, repeating weeks 10 to 14 while adding a few repeats each month and racing at 12K and 10 miles. Longer runs give you greater endurance though, so do at least increase to a monthly 14.

15	Race 10K	11	7 / 4.5	10	39
16	10 x 400	14	32 / 4.0	11	39.5
17	8 x 600	15	8 / 5.0	12	42.5
18	20 x 200	16	28 / 4.0	10	40.5
19	10 x 300	12	4 / 2.5	7	31.5
20	Race 12K	12	28 / 4.0	10	41

Most runners should then consolidate by repeating weeks 16 to 20. When you feel ready, move up to week:

21	12 x 400	17	8 / 5.0	12	45
22	8 x 600	18	24 / 4.0	12	45
23	20 x 200	18	8 / 5.0	10	44
24	12 x 300	14	24 / 3.0	8	35.5

25 Race 10 miles:

Because you've just done a long run in the form of the 10-mile race, it is probably best to run only 5 miles the next day. Two gentle fartlek sessions with 3 miles at speed on days four and six will give you a 33 mile week, and sets you up nicely to repeat weeks 21 to 24 prior to your first half-marathon race. If your next half-marathon course is flat, consider replacing one of the hill sessions with a 5K race.

Naturally, if your typical weeks training when you start is similar to say week 12...this is where you join the party. You'll be ready for a 10-mile race after a dozen weeks.

Half-marathon goal pace.

Take the soft option for your first couple of halfs. Double your 10K time and add eleven minutes. Run even pace, and the first 6 miles should feel easy. You'll be running mere seconds per mile faster than the middle section of your midweek run, 30 seconds per mile slower than 10K pace, and much slower than in your fartlek training.

The remaining 7 miles is mental practice for future half marathon racing. These miles aren't fast, but some sections will feel harsh. Stay relaxed, maintain form, be positive and sustain your pace to the finish. You'll race the half-marathon faster in the future. Don't hurt too much in your first few half-marathons.

35 to 45 miles per week too tame? If you're already doing two cross training sessions, you can add an additional run at any stage, but be consistent. Did a 4 miler twice a week plus week one's training? By week 16 an easy 7 could be a rest day: or, it might take until week 16 before you add a fifth run...of only three miles. Do what works for you. Whatever mileage you're doing, you still get your finishers medal and the satisfaction from your first half marathon.

You don't have take 30 weeks to reach your first half marathon. *Runner's World* April 2,002 gave an 8 week half marathon training schedule. It is probably available on their web site, but note the following weaknesses.

* No hills. None for beginners; none for advanced runners.
* Beginners don't do a single race before the half marathon, and they do no speed running, yet they are the people who benefit the most from practice with both.
* The longest run for all levels is 7 days before the half marathon, yet it takes 14 to 21 days to get training benefits from running. Seven days pre race should be 4 miles shorter than your longest run, not one mile longer.
* No cross training for intermediate or advanced runners.
* Advanced runners race a 10K at the end of week two, suggesting that they are fit. Yet, their interval sessions at 5K pace are only 1.5 to 2 miles for the first three out of the 8 weeks. They should have been doing 4 mile interval sessions to qualify as advanced runners, yet they are knocked back to a beginners Interval session.

This author suggests you stick with a sensible build up over at least 12 to 24 weeks, and rest up for your races.

Chapter Four

Recovery from Quality Running & Injury Prevention

Misguided people think that we run with our legs. Sensible people use their heads.

Training faster (easy to define) or training harder (the definition is more subtle), is rarely the best way to improve your half-marathon time. To run faster at any distance you must train sensibly, within your own body's potential: you must train long enough, but often enough to improve, yet short enough and seldom enough to recover.

Fail to recover and you'll be forced to run slower in future sessions. Fail to recover and you risk staleness and injuries.

Bill Bowerman, who coached the successful University of Oregon team, which included multiple American record breaker Steve Prefontaine, called this the hard training easy training approach. You place a series of easy days or runs after each hard training session to allow your body to become stronger: during this recovery phase, your muscles get stronger due to the stimulus from that hard training session.

Ph.D.s would rather quote scientifics than brilliant coaches, so lets look at a model which is somewhat less attractive than Cindy Crawford to tell us how to train.

Yakovlev's rather curvy model stipulates that if your initial training session is too hard for you at your current fitness level, your fatigue level from it will be too severe. You will take so long to recover from one session that you cannot improve your fitness.

Yakovlev's model also states that if you try to train hard again before your body has recovered from the initial session, you're doomed to failure due to muscle fatigue. Wait the right length of time after session one and your muscles will be in better shape than before session one, and you'll be able to train hard again. In fact, you'll be able to train a bit harder than last time.

Sadly, by Yakovlev's model, if you wait too long after the first session, you'll also perform no better or possibly worse than before the first session. The key then is to repeat the session at the peak of your recovery, or when you have completely recovered from the initial training session. The tricky part is knowing what works for you.

Yet, by training at 5K or 15K pace for speed sessions you can avoid running them too fast. By restricting yourself to 10 percent of your weekly mileage in one session, and by restricting yourself to mere quarter mile increments when increasing the volume of speed running, you should avoid excessive periods of fatigue or overtraining.

Muscle soreness is from micro muscle fiber tears. They will heal with sufficient rest, and the repaired muscles will be stronger. You will be fitter and run faster at all distances.

Perhaps the best use of Yakovlev's model is to gradually increase the volume or the speed of your quality days. The full training adaptation runners are looking for takes weeks or months to show itself in faster race times. However, build up to 10 times 400 meters at your current 5K pace, and that session will gradually feel easier. Your muscles will adapt and your running mechanics will improve. Then, after doing the session several times you'll be ready to:

* Add a repeat or two; or
* Run a second per interval faster; or
* Run 600s instead of 400s; or
* Take less time for your recovery.

Note: less time for the recovery could mean 60 seconds instead of 90 between repeats, or taking only two easy days instead of three easy days prior to the next quality session.

In most circumstances, you also have to avoid training too easily. Initially, your speed sessions had to be easy to get your muscles and lungs used to running quite fast. After a few days of easy and sometimes long runs, you did another little bout of fast running to learn the nuances of running at 5K pace or 15K pace. Then you did longer sessions such as mile repeats at 15K pace and 300s and 400-meter intervals at 5K pace.

The litmus test which this writer uses to define a session which is too hard is: can you run 12 to 15 miles the day after a speed running day? Of course, long run pace is 60 to 90 seconds per mile slower than half-marathon race pace.

Without the endurance from long runs, you're a lost cause at the half-marathon. The combination of speed and long runs should then be followed by sufficient easy sessions to prepare you for your second speed run of the week or 10 day cycle, followed by your second long run.

Recovery from hard sessions.

Tips to speed your recovery and adaptation from hard sessions and to decrease DOMS (see also page 82).

1. Run at the right speed for you and at the right speed for you this week. Coming back from a lay-off? Run slower than you did before your lay-off. Current 5K to 15K pace.
2. Run the right quantity of quality. Training volume is the main factor for improving performance. Achieve that volume on a fairly frequent and very consistent basis. But do 10 percent of current mileage fairly fast twice a week.

3. Nourishment. Liquids and food speed your ability to recover from harsh work-bouts. Complex carbohydrates plus a bit of protein and plenty of liquids will replenish your glycogen stores, prevent muscle breakdown and maintain blood plasma volume (prevent dehydration) respectively. Semi-liquid foods such as yogurt and smoothies are perfect for recovery snacks. Consume three snacks at two hourly intervals after your interval sessions and long runs.

4. Physical rest and sleep. After soaking your muscles in cold water for 5 to 10 minutes, put your feet up while you consume the first snack. Then take your warm shower and gently massage sore spots. Repeat the cold immersion later and Jacuzzi briefly on big training days. Tough training days are not the ideal day to do a major yard project, though it may be a good day for an afternoon siesta. Get your nightly 7 to 9 hours of sleep on a regular basis to rest your muscles and your mind.

5. Recovery exercise brings nutrient rich blood into your fatigued muscles. It could mean two miles at easy pace for the warmdown, followed by half a mile of walking as you rehydrate. Try another mile of walking six hours after your training run. Recovery exercise will probably include a 5-mile easy run the next day. Recovery exercise may be 8 times one mile at anaerobic threshold the day after doing 16 x 400 meters 5K pace, followed by 18 miles the next day, then an easy five to rest up for the next quality session.

6. Racing generally requires more rest though. Racing at 10K to the half-marathon requires 6 to 13 days of easy exercise before attempting serious training again. One mile of racing usually requires one restive day of exercise to recover, or about two weeks for half-marathon recovery. Been used to 20 x 400 meters at 2-mile race pace in training before your race? 12 x 400 at 5K pace would be an easy day

of running. It's still prudent to wait until four or five days after the race before running at 5K pace; only do so if you are well experienced, and experiencing minimal aches and fatigue from the prior race.

Many runners find that doing 5Ks and 10Ks weekly allows for complete recovery between races. They require a minimal speed session midweek to stay relaxed and can improve for 10 to 12 weeks at a variety of distances. They are actually working with Yakovlev's model. They are resting and doing just enough running to achieve ever-increasing performances each weekend. Most people then need a long period at base training.

7. <u>Do striders at the end of easy runs</u>.
Two to three times each week, run some 50 to 150 meter striders on smooth dirt, grass or a track at the end of easy runs. These are not speed sessions, so you must not feel tired after this minute or two of fast running.

How fast to run? Stride out gently, then pick up speed over 50 meters to reach 5K to 2 mile pace. Hold for another 50 meters then decelerate. Take a full rest and repeat in the opposite direction. Start with two efforts but don't make it an effort to run because relaxation is paramount. Add a pair of striders each month until you reach 8 or 10.

Use a quick leg turnover with quick arms back and forward to keep your legs going fast. Keep these striders short: run a maximum of 150 meters each time. This is not a workout. Save your legs for the 4 times one mile tomorrow! Striders stimulate your neural pathways, thus improving your neuromuscular coordination. Running muscles become more coordinated or fluid, and you will waste less energy.

Keep your actual stride length short too because taking short strides with low impact decreases your injury risk. At all cost, avoid the clumping from overstriding and from running with poor form toward the end of long runs and speed sessions. Use short strides and keep your feet close to the ground to reduce jarring.

Overstriding costs you because:

* Running efficiency is decreased while
* Ground impact is increased.

Both are bad news for runners. The visit to a doctor will cost you money; the forced break from running will set back your fitness and ruin your half marathon plans.

Speed running with friends.

Running with speedy people is fraught with overtraining potential. Run at the right pace for you or you'll defeat Yakovlev's model because you run too fast: run no faster than your 2-mile race pace. See pages 93 to 99.

Run fast once a week by yourself for self-reliance, but run fast with friends once a week for your toughest speed session. Friends make the middle part of 800s or 600s feel easier because you don't have to set the pace on all repeats.

You still have to monitor the pace though. Get pulled along too fast and you'll suffer for the rest of the session. Linger 10 or 20 meters behind the pace setter on any repeat which your friends miss-judge. Saying, "Ease back" or "Too fast" will usually set them straight in the first 50 to 100 meters of an interval. If they don't correct their pace, let them go and cruise in at your correct pace.

Friends will make you less likely to cut a session short. You will consistently run your three or four miles of repeats if training with others. Got a cold or had a tough few days at work? Walk and take a drink while the group does its fifth and ninth repeat so as not to over stress yourself.

If you're the only one resting up for a race the following week, you'll probably do only half of the speed session. But this would be a planned half session. Time your training partners for the remainder of the session while you do an early warmdown.

Make sure that you decide on the session for next week before leaving the current days running. This allows you to look forward to say mile repeats at 5K pace; it also allows you to prepare for the mile repeats by running solo 200s at 2 mile pace three days before the mile repeats which you've planned. Hint: If your next group session is 400s at 2-mile pace, your session three days prior might be long repeats at 15K pace.

Make sure you do sufficient warmup prior to speed running. One mile and a couple of striders is enough for some runners; two miles is too short for other runners. Do your stretches, then 4 to 8 striders before your first of 4 to 16 repeats. Striders before speed running:

* Flood your muscles with nutrient rich blood;
* Get your fast-twitch muscle fibers ready for action;
* Stimulate your muscles and mind to race pace;
* Puts your muscles through the range of motion which is required to attain race pace.

Run the first lap a second or two slower than goal pace for the day. When doing long repeats, ease up to goal pace by the third or fourth lap. With mile repeats at 6-minute miles or 90 seconds per lap, run a 92 second lap, then ease up to 91 and two at 90 seconds to give a 6.03 mile. Do the second repeat at a steady 90 seconds per lap, and run no faster than 89 seconds for any lap thereafter. With short repeats, run the entire first repeat 8 to 10 seconds per mile slower than goal pace, and ease up to goal pace by the fourth repeat.

Time yourself. The first runner across the finish line times his or her own repeat, eases to a jog in a straight line away from the finish, and into lane four to leave the inside lane for other groups doing speedwork. He will not be able to clock you in because he will be 15 meters away if you are 6 seconds slower. He will be walking or jogging slowly and waiting for you and others to rejoin the group. Clock your own time as you cross the line, jog on up to meet with the group, and then prepare for the next repetition.

Heartrate Monitors.

Running must feel very easy for it to do us much good. Long runs must be done at closer to 60 % of our maximum heart rate (MHR) than 80 %. 15K or 10 mile pace for anaerobic threshold improvement is only 80 % of MHR in our early years and 86 to 92 % of MHR when we're fully trained running machines. VO2 max and running economy is best improved at a mere 95 % of MHR, or 5K race pace, with minimal amounts at 2-mile race pace or 97 to 98 % of MHR. How do you measure workout intensity?

Heart-rate monitors give an additional guide to judge workout intensity, plus an early warning system for fatigue, dehydration and other ills. Monitors give an objective and accurate feedback about how your body is performing at a given pace on a given day. On some days, the heartrate monitor is a better guide than your subjective feelings about how hard you are working. Running can feel harder on stressful days, yet your monitor will not be fooled. If you ease off by 10 seconds per mile, the lower alarm limit will beep you alert, reminding you to pick up the pace. Don't become a slave to the monitor though. You still have to decide if you'd like a lower training pace on these days.

Your upper HR alarm will beep at slower than usual pace if your body is sick or overtrained. Run at the slower pace, but also decrease the duration of the run to avoid overtraining and to prepare the body for its bout of the cold. You may already know you're off-color. Use the monitor to set the pace for a few days.

Heartrate monitor training pace is still dictated by a percentage of your MHR. This way of calculating MHR, which is taken from my trusty copy of _Running Dialogue,_ also factors in your resting HR:

(200 minus HR at rest) x % training effort today + HR at rest
Example: HR at rest 80, and wishing to train at 60 % effort.
(200 - 80) x 60 % add 80
(120 x 60 %) + 80
72 + 80 = 152 or a training threshold easily reached by the unfit person. Here are that person's other HR goals.

* 164 at 70 % of max HR
* 176 at 80 % of max HR
* 188 at 90 %
* 194 at 95 %
* 200 at 100 %

Substitute your HR at rest to get your base HR for easy runs. Example: a 60 HR at rest person will train at a steady 144 beats per minute during most of his or her mileage. Top of the range for steady mileage is 70 % of MHR so:
(200 - 60) x 70 % and add 60 gives 158 for the upper alarm.
FYI: Other goal HRs if your resting HR is 60:

* 172 at 80 % of max HR
* 186 at 90 %
* 193 at 95 %
* 200 at 100 %

The joy of this formula is that you can adjust your HR training range every time your resting HR goes down 2 to 4 beats on a consistent basis. Had a long layoff? Calculate your HR goals on your now faster resting HR.

Prefer MHR based on age? Runner's World October 2,001 issue shows the formula: 205 - (.5 x age). A 50 year olds MHR would be 180 if running for the first time since grade school: it would also be 180 if racing his or her 50th half-marathon!

The best MHR predictor is a field test at maximum speed. It is prudent to be very fit before attempting this test or you'll find yourself in hospital or heaven.

Warm-up with about two miles at gentle pace. After stretching, run three or four striders of about 100 meters. Then, run all-out for 60 to 90 seconds. If you've been exercising for several years, do this up a hill. After a rest, run all-out again, but pace yourself to reach total exhaustion at the end of the fast section. If you reach exhaustion midway, you'll be running slower at the end, and the lower reading from the heartrate test will mislead you into a slower pace (at which) to do your steady runs.

At the point of maximum exhaustion, read your heartrate monitor. Or, check your pulse for ten seconds, and then multiply by six. The number will either be your maximum heartrate (MHR), or the maximum level at which your body or pain threshold allows you to exercise. Try a third repeat to see if you can get your heartrate higher.

Most books would now give a slew of workouts based on MHR. However, Chapter 7 and 8 give you dozens of sessions at these intensities because you'll be training at 15K to 5K pace for most of your speed running. That is, at 80 to 95 % of MHR. Do your:

* Easy runs and long runs at 60 to 75 % of your MHR
* Tempo or Anaerobic Threshold at 86 to 92 % of MHR
* Intervals or VO2 Max training at 95 to 98 % of MHR

In a quirk of running efficiency, 15K pace or 10 mile pace will take some of you up to 92 percent of your MHR and stimulate your anaerobic threshold and your running economy. In addition to the above, the ideal training heartrates are suggested by your HR in a race. Namely:

* 5K pace is at 95 to 97 % of MHR
* 10K pace is 92 to 94 %
* Half-marathon pace is 85 to 88 %

Note: 10K pace typically will be 92 to 94 % of MHR. 10K pace trains your anaerobic threshold, but you'd be better off running a bit slower; 10K pace also trains your VO2 max system. You get a double training effect at this middle ground of 92 to 94 percent of MHR. 10K pace is also about 90 percent of your VO2 maximum, a superb intensity to train at using long repeats (see page 157).

Two-mile race pace will be close to 98 percent of your MHR and there's little point in running faster. You can't maintain 100 percent of MHR for long enough to make any significant training gains. Two-mile race pace is also 100 percent of VO2 max. While it's impossible to train higher than your MHR, you can train at greater than 100 percent of your VO2 maximum. As with training at close to MHR, you cannot train at greater than VO2 max for very long periods.

Running 200 and 300 meter repeats faster than mile race pace takes you close to your MHR and to over 110 percent of your VO2 max, and deeply into oxygen debt. The main purpose of these short reps is to improve your ability to run while in severe oxygen debt or to run anaerobically.

Fine if you want to race a mile? But your goal is to race the half-marathon. Most of your speed training will be at 15K to 5K race pace, or at 86 to 95 percent of your MHR.

It is a good idea to take a few weeks of low mileage once a year for muscle recovery or healing. However, no running for three weeks will decrease:

* Your hearts' stroke volume by 10 %
* Your muscles' oxidative enzyme activity
* Your muscles' ability to store glycogen by 40 %
* Your blood volume and capillaries:

Or, your VO2 max will decrease! You'll add a minute to your 5K, and several extra minutes for a half marathon.

Run a few one mile repeats at your old 5K pace twice a week, and you can keep almost all of your old fitness. 50 mile per week runners will need 5 repeats (10 % of old mileage). Add the warmup and cooldown and you've got 16 miles per week, or a saving of about 99 miles over 3 weeks.

Chapter Five

More Injury Prevention Tips

High mileage and long runs are the most reliable predictors of injury. Half-marathon runners are clearly at high injury risk, which is one of the reasons for the numerous low mileage survival training programs that take a person to long races on three or four runs per week.

As Runner's World columnist Joe Henderson wrote recently, "injuries usually result from training mistakes--running too far, too fast, too often."

Poor planning is the number two injury risk predictor. If you stretch properly and regularly, increase your mileage and quality running in a logical and gentle way, the 45 mile per week runner should experience no more injuries than the 25 mile per week runner.

The real injury problem is with beginner runners because distance training requires restraint, which is something new runners often take a while to learn.

Start any exercise program gently. It's no accident that children learn to walk before they run: So should you. Train for and race 5Ks for a year, then spend a year concentrating on the 10K. Spend an entire year training to race the half-marathon, while also racing a few 5K and 10Ks, and you'll even be ready to embark on a 20 week training program for a 30K race with minimal injury risk.

Olympics are every four years. Build up slowly and make gentle transitions from sloth to recreational runner, to competent 5K runner, to proficient 10K runner, to accomplished half-marathon runner.

Golden Rules to avoid Injury:

No sudden mileage changes. The 10 percent rule says you can add up to 10 percent each week. You can double your mileage in 8 weeks. However, there is even less injury risk if you drop back 5 % once every 4 weeks. Give your muscles the chance to heal and become stronger. It still only takes 12 weeks to move from 20 to 40 miles. Stay at the new level for 6 months before moving up again.

Want a different plan and running 20 miles per week at present? Adding two miles each week would take you up to 40 in ten weeks. Better still, when you've reached 30 miles, stay a few weeks while converting one of those miles to quality running every other week.

If you were running two miles of short repeats at 5K pace once a week when training at 20 miles per week, gradually increase the session to 3 miles. Were you also running 3 miles at 20 to 30 seconds per mile slower than 5K pace once a week previously? Increase toward 4 miles of tempo pace running or intervals. Every other week, run hills instead of one of those sessions!

When you're doing 7 miles, or 25 % of mileage as quality running each week, chances are good that you're also ready for the second mileage increase to 40, but take another 5 weeks to get there. Note that the ten percent rule would allow you to go from 30 to 40 miles in just three weeks, but what's your rush? High school runners should add 5 to 10 weekly miles per year to reach their maximum mileage in their mid to late 20s, their racing peak. For you, a one-third mileage increase from 30 over 5 weeks is plenty fast enough, then increase your quality sessions by a quarter mile every two weeks to reach 4 miles at speed two or three times per week. Chapter Three is even more conservative.

Had several weeks rest as prescribed on page 55? Start week one of your comeback at 75 % of old mileage, and reach full mileage in week five.

Wear running shoes for your running. Specialist running store salespeople are great for advice...if they are runners. There is no need to spend $100 for a pair of running shoes. My local Big 5 employs at least two sub 15-minute 5K runners, and every week, several types of running shoe are discounted. Last years model does not have this years technical monstrosity to ruin a perfect shoe! I have rarely paid over $40 per pair.

Buy your shoes when your feet are fully expanded, that is, late in the day. Wear your running socks and bring any shoe inserts that you use. Get your feet measured and make sure that your heels fit snugly. On the other hand, your toes need space to spread out, and a half-inch or more at the end of the big toe for movement. Give the shoes a test run.

Break in each new pair of running shoes. Shoes change your running form in many ways. Your new pair may correct 90 percent of your overpronation, but your muscles may only be used to 80 percent of it being corrected. Do two or three short runs in new shoes before you use them for speed sessions or long runs. Buy the shoes two to four weeks before you'll need them for an important long run.

Never run long or race in brand new shoes. If you like racing shoes, wear them for one speed session *every* week to keep your feet and muscles used to them.

Wear the best shoes for the job. A shoe which weighs one ounce less than your usual training shoe has the potential to save you about one second per mile. However, lighter shoes have less cushioning and stability, which may cost you more than that one second per mile. You'll have to practice running in the lightweight shoes to get used to them, to get used to your changed biomechanics, which help you to run faster. Use them for a full session of speed running while monitoring for unwanted motion in the last third of the session.

Going from 12 ounce training shoes to 7 ounce racers can get you 30 seconds off of your 10K and a minute from your half-marathon...provided they don't cause an injury which sidelines you for weeks. Sore Achilles and strained calves often occur from the lower heels on racing shoes.

A sensible compromise is lightweight trainers, which will save a few ounces yet give you most of the support. Racing shoes are great up to the 10K; lightweight runners and runners with a light touch when they bump back into contact with the ground, may find that racing shoes are supportive enough for the half-marathon.

Dump stiff or worn-out running shoes. Wear flexible yet supportive shoes. Most running shoes will last 400 miles. If you're overweight or land heavily due to overstriding, your shoe life will be shorter. One trick is to run your first 200 miles for each pair on the road or track or for your long runs. Then relegate them to soft surface runs on grass or dirt trails. Keep three to four pairs on the go at different wear levels. Watch for:

* The middle part of the shoe (aptly named the midsole) cracked or brittle. It is not as supportive as in its heyday.

* The upper leans to the inside or outside. Leaning to the inside after very few miles, with the midsole bashed in are signs of overpronation. You'll need shoes that are more protective.

* Muscle aches suggestive of injury are more likely to happen if you only use one pair of running shoes. Some runners don't get new shoes until something hurts. Proactive shoe rotation and buying is better. For your three to four pair rotation, choose shoes with slightly different features. Overpronate? All your shoes need to protect you and stabilize your feet, but you can still use different levels of protection.

* Due to better quality materials, noticeable wearing off of the tread design on the bottom of the shoe is not reliable.

Don't neglect the socks you wear. Well-padded sport socks can increase your running comfort and cut down on fatigue and blisters, but are no substitute for good shoes.

Arch supports, padding, sorbothane inserts or prescription orthotics can make your shoes closer to perfect for your running style.

Orthotics should usually be semi-flexible and full length for the best results. You may not need them for all of your mileage. Some running shoes do not have removable inserts, making orthotic use difficult. If the shoe suits you, if it corrects most of your pronation or supination, doing one third of your mileage in them may balance you nicely to do the rest of your training in orthotic friendly shoes.

Stay off the sidewalk because it's usually concrete, and at six times harder than asphalt it's the worst running surface made by man. You also have to jump down every 100 to 200 yards at cross streets with numerous 2-ton murderous weapons crossing your path! Pedestrians can also be a problem until they become runners.

Avoid roads with a slope or camber: they force one foot to overpronate while the other foot over supinates. Running tracks are fine to get you up to your first two-mile run, but then find dirt trails, parks, grass and some nice flat asphalt. Watch for sprinklers when running on grass.

New to running at 42? You will not race as fast as you could have at age 32, but it might take you 5 years to perfect your exercise skills and endurance for running. You'll get five years of PRs if PRs are important to you. Then you can look forward to hitting 50, a chance to race those tiring 54 year olds, on whom you have a 2 percent performance allowance courtesy of a better VO2 max and stronger muscles because you're a young 50 to 54 athlete.

High mileage requires more rest days. You get a greater training affect from one 10-mile run than from two 5s. However, you're more likely to need a rest day after a 10-mile run than after a 5. The rest day can be a three-mile run, thus you get 13 in two days. The rest day could also be a gentle cross training day.

High mileage runners may consider an 8 mile run at 70 percent of their maximum heartrate to be a rest day: Low mileage runners will consider that eight to be a harsh run!

Long runs build your leg strength, and you need strong legs to run fast. During extra runs and extra mileage, keep your pace slow with a low shuffling stride to reduce injury risk, and to make your running more efficient. Your muscles adapt quite rapidly, while your tendons, ligaments and joints adapt and grow stronger very slowly. You cannot run when injured, so increase your mileage gradually.

However, you become inefficient when fatigued. Your ability to absorb impact shock decreases toward the end of your runs. It starts with foot placement, but you need to concentrate on all aspects of your running form when tired. If you have aching quadriceps toward the end of your runs, you're probably not using your calf muscles enough.

Overstriding is your enemy...you're unable to control excessive movements...placing strain on fatigued muscles. Think leg turnover once or twice every mile, and when attempting to run fast. Land softly, as if onto eggshells, with short strides to decrease calf muscle, hamstring muscles, Achilles tendon and knee insults.

Don't get too ambitious. Your long run should rarely be more than one third of your weekly mileage. The speed element of an individual speed session should rarely be more than ten percent of your weekly miles. Speedwork should rarely be faster than 5K race pace. Speed running during your long runs should be restricted to race pace or a bit slower, which means about one minute per mile faster than your average long run pace.

You will often need to break this rule, but generally, don't run longer than ten miles more than once a week. If you want 12 miles on Wednesday, five in the morning and seven in the evening is less taxing and reduces injury risk from poor running form in the last miles of a 12. However, do warm up and stretch for both runs, and keep the pace reasonable. If you're aiming for 70 percent of maximum heartrate, stay at that pace for both runs because you'll be running speedwork the next day. Split the runs by at least six hours, and eat and hydrate after each run.

Many runners prefer their two runs in a day to be on speed days. A relaxing short run in the morning loosens up their muscles for the evening speed or quality session.

Avoid Overtraining by not running too often.
See also Chapter Four. Some runners train 14 times per week, accumulating over a hundred miles most weeks. Research shows that you achieve most aerobic benefits on 60 miles per week. Don't let rest days frighten you. As you age, you'll need more rest each week, and rest days allow you to train better over the following days.

Monitor your running form: The most successful runners at all levels monitor their running form and pace at all times. Drift through a range of thoughts and discussions while running, but monitor your form and pace every half a mile. Pay attention to what your entire body is doing.

Tuning into your body helps you to run faster. You need to practice it in training, during speedwork, and especially in the second half of long runs.

Watch for running surface changes that require you to make speed changes. Decide how much effort to put into a hill or favorite stretch of the trail if you are changing speeds. Otherwise, maintain an even effort as you visualize running a great race. Compare your breathing, legspeed, arm carriage and running intensity to what you've done in the past: Use your watch, speed and fellow runners as a secondary guide to your effort level.

Follow the hard/easy principle. Long runs or hard speed sessions are generally followed by an easy day. However, a sensible speed session should precede your weekend long run. If 16 times 400 meters leaves you wiped out for three days, it's too hard for you. Restrict yourself to manageable speed sessions, which allow you to run at least 10 to 12 miles with ease the next day.

If you have a non-physical job, do some low intensity exercise such as easy walking or cycling on your rest days from running.

But, run very easily on your restive days. Running at 60 to 70 percent of your maximum heartrate is training, yet it rests you up for your two or three faster or longer runs each week. You should breath in for three steps, then out for three steps. This is conversational pace, because you're able to talk easily while training. Running faster than 70 percent max HR will not make you fitter. Save your muscles for the days they are supposed to be training at 85 to 95 percent of maximum heartrate.

Start all runs slowly by easing into your runs. Do five minutes of gentle stretching before exiting the door. The older you are, the more time your connective tissue takes to warm up and to get ready for running. Therefore, walk a few hundred feet, and then run slowly. Once your muscles are warmed up, edge up closer toward training speed for the day. The second mile could be 10 to 15 seconds slower than goal pace, and then you'll hit goal pace with warm muscles and a relaxed mindset. For hills and other speed running, see Chapters Three, Seven and Eight.

Gentle massage and stretching speeds up your recovery while loosening tight muscles. Studies show that a quality massage can reduce muscle soreness, tension and swelling. Muscle relaxation is one component needed for running. Get yourself kneaded to:

* Prepare for a time trial or key interval session that is two to three weeks prior to your main race.
* To aid recovery two days after your key session.
* Between hard sessions to enable you to train hard once every three days instead of once every four days.

The massage should be gentle if it is on the first day post session or one day prior to harsh workouts. To get the full benefit, follow the massage with stretching. To avoid damaging fragile tissues, restrict deeper tissue massage to two to three days either side of harsh sessions. Tell the therapist where your aches are and don't let him or her hurt you…yet allow them to work gently on your sensitive spots.

Don't consider the cost of a pair of running shoes for a massage an appropriate investment? Self-massage of calves, shins and the thigh muscles is easy. Knead your way *up* the muscle. When you find a sore spot, rub it gently horizontally (cross-fiber massage). Massaging sore spots with ice works nicely, especially the day of your workout.

Keep your muscles balanced--don't overuse any type of training. Practice the art of maintaining balance by...Standing with your feet close together. Lift one foot a few inches off the ground and balance for up to 30 seconds. Then practice with your other foot. When you can do this with your arms crossed, do two to three sets and then practice with your eyes closed. Balance exercises train the sensors in your joints...which should then make faster adjustments when you run.

Had your fortieth birthday more than seven days ago? It's time for weight training. Your fifth decade is when you begin to lose significant muscle strength, and you also increase injury risk from running nearly every day. Solve both problems by weight training instead of running for one more session per week than in your thirties.

* You'll exercise some muscles which you don't exercise very much or often while running;
* You'll strengthen muscles which you do use while running; and,
* Protect yourself from injury because there is no jarring.

Before weight training, warm up with ten minutes of biking or elliptical training, then stretch. Cool off with 10 minutes of exercise as you did for your warm up, then follow it with 20 minutes of pool running, and you've got yourself a cardiovascular session too. But don't workout...this month. Keep the intensity low to rest up for the next days run.

Do 10 to 12 different exercises. Lift and push light weights for at least the first two months. Lift 10 to 12 repeats of a weight you would be able to lift for 15 reps. When your muscles have begun to adapt, lift a weight which you could lift 12 times without pain, but lift it 10 times. Graduate to 8 reps of a weight that would completely exhaust you at 10 reps. Then ease up to two sets and ease back up to 10 to 12 repeats as your work capacity increases. See also pages 108 to 147.

Cardiovascular Cross training decreases injury risk and aids recovery from harsh training runs. An hours bike ride relaxes and lengthens your hamstrings, and adds strength to your quadriceps. Prefer a more weight bearing exercise? The elliptical trainer is essentially non-impact, yet you're on your feet! Prefer zero impact? Water running fits the bill. Cross training burns calories, relieves stress and gets you fit before you move your running mileage up again. Cross training decreases your injury risk, especially in your later decades.

Warmdown: At the end of all runs, cruise easily at 60 percent of maximum heartrate for 10 minutes. This is the cooldown or warmdown. It's as vital after 4 miles of hard running, as it is after 14 miles of steady running. Finish with an additional few minutes of walking to:

* Reduce blood pooling & help your muscles to recover faster, plus:
* Speed your immune system's recovery, including
* Better white blood cell counts.
* And to savor the moment, that post coital, I mean post run feeling.

Stretch before all speed running and stretch again after a relaxing shower. Avoid excessive stretching with fatigued muscles just after a hard session. See pages 70-82.

Run fast every week, especially during base building. Sixteen relaxed striders at 5K pace is a pleasant change from that important yet humdrum mileage. Bounding for 30 seconds across deep sand half a dozen times adds strength to your muscles and improves VO2 max. Hill repeats are the usual winter background training.

Don't ignore your bounding and striders at any time of the year. Run your gliders or striders on a weekly basis. Shorten your stride while increasing leg turnover only slightly. Keep your feet close to the ground as you whip your legs through to gain leg speed. Run lightly...as if you're on hot sand or ice. Run relaxed and tall. Do not tense up.

Move your arms back and forward sufficiently to stop your shoulders from rolling. Most people need to bend their elbows to 90 degrees; few people benefit from bringing their hands across their chest. Arms should generally go straight back and straight forward. When you're looking ahead, you should not see your hands. If you do see your hands, they are probably too high. Arms are for balance, not for propelling you forward. You're not a sprinter, so don't run like one. Upper body tension travels down to your propulsive leg muscles. Stay loose above the waist.

Vary your steady running pace day by day. All running at slower than half-marathon pace or all running at faster than race pace will cause early fatigue with sore muscles. Incorporate plenty of running at 1 to 2 minutes per mile slower than half marathon pace. Too much slow running makes you unable to handle the mental concentration of fast running, so aim for up to 25 percent of your miles to be at 15K pace or faster.

The law of diminishing returns for running states that each additional mile of steady running, or increase in speed running will actually result in a decrease in running performance and an increased injury risk. It's called overtraining. Sometimes, you'll want to find out how hard you can train without getting injured. Taking yourself to the verge of injury is risky. Listen to those achy muscles and act on their message. Slow down or reduce mileage.

Once a year, and for several weeks, run the minimum which allows you to stay healthy. Forty minutes of exercise, 5 times per week with a couple of miles of fast running on two of those days at 5K pace keeps your heart and other muscles healthy.

Sickness requires an easier run or rest. If your temperature is above 100 degrees Fahrenheit, you should probably rest. When ill, train less intensely and for fewer miles. Your muscles are more prone to injury when you're ill, but gentle exercise increases your sense of well-being, plus it stimulates release of Human Growth Hormone and body healing. An easy run helps clear out your sinuses when you have a cold. You rarely need to take an entire week off from running.

Ice or cool your muscles in a natural body of water to aid training recovery. Hose your legs to decrease inflammation. Hours later, when you've rehydrated, may be Jacuzzi time. Heat can make post exercise soreness worse if used too close to the exercise session. If the run was particularly harsh, keep to short dips in the hot stuff, followed by cold water dips and gentle stretching. The jets and the heat help to loosen you up...your joints and your individual muscle cells relax.

Four time New York Marathon winner Alberto Salazar, has been quoted as saying, "Never ask your body to do something in a race that it hasn't done in training - and you'll have the confidence that you can actually do it." (I would add "injury free" to the end of his sentence).

* Practice 10 mile runs at marathon pace before your half-marathons.
* Practice 15 to 18 mile steady runs slower than marathon pace before the 20-mile race.

* Practice running at or faster than half marathon pace for 5-mile sessions, which are broken into sections (as 5K to 15K pace intervals).

For race day, rest up and run even pace while focusing on running form, and you should get through most races without injury. Races require that you put your body on the line. There's a risk that part of your body will break. Typically, the break happens days or weeks after the race because you don't allow sufficient time for your body to recover after an all out race.

Stay hydrated to reduce injury risk. Stay well nourished too. You only need 90 grams of protein, but you also need iron, zinc, vitamin C and many other nutrients to have your best chance at avoiding injury. See the detailed nutrition advice in Best Marathons.

Heartrate monitors can track distance and speed. Using the global tracking system, supped up monitors can calculate your distance. The watch section records the time which you run, so the combination of distance and time gives you an accurate pace per mile. Running 4 to 15 minute repeats on a trail? Your device will calculate pace to within one percent, or within 5 seconds per mile for an 8:20 per mile session.

Still got sore muscles? Stop the overtraining! Sorry. You need to get your muscles somewhat sore on some days. Soreness lingering for days? Injuries could be imminent. If muscle soreness eases after warming up, and does not affect your running form, easy running can speed your recovery.

Try a cheap massage. Buy a foam cylinder and roll your muscles over it. Excellent for the I-T band, gluteals, quadriceps, hamstrings and calf muscles, and it makes a change from using your hands. More details at www.smiweb.org and www.optp.com

Chapter Six

Stretching & Mobility

"You cannot train when you are injured."
Almost an Olympian before he learned about regular stretching.

The American Council on Exercise says there are three important types of exercise: aerobic activity, muscular strengthening and flexibility. Chapter Three gives you more than enough aerobic activity for health, Chapter Nine will give you weight training, and this chapter will show you how to stretch safely for fitness.

Half Marathon fitness requires training, but you can't train properly for the Half if you're always injured. Stretching before and after running helps prevent injury, while also improving race performance by increasing your range of motion and coordination.

Flexibility will improve your running. Regular stretching maintains your flexibility, your balance and loosens your joints. Stretching reduces muscular tension and improves circulation...allowing you to train with more miles or to train with harder miles (or a bit of each).

Muscles are 10 percent shorter than normal when you wake up; they are 10 percent longer than usual after warming up. Muscles work better when they are long--they exert the same amount of force with less effort: You'll conserve energy to run farther at a given pace.

Injuries delay peak performances because you take long periods away from your sport. When coming back from injury it may only take a few weeks to regain most of your aerobic fitness and the ability to run well at threshold pace or modest speeds. You can also run well at mile pace for short bursts: But it takes months to regain your full strength and the ability to run fast for long periods.

Basic Stretching Tips.

Stretch often: Do at least 10 minutes for every run and at least 15 minutes on non-running days. Only got 20 minutes to run this morning, so you'll do the remaining 20 minutes after work? Tough. You'll need two 10-minute sessions of stretching. Get organized for a continuous 40 minutes of running for more endurance and you'll only need 10 minutes total for your stretches. A few stretches later will help too!

Stretch before and after running. Post run stretching decreases cramping, muscle tightness and the reduced range of motion that can occur with muscle fatigue.

Warm up for a few minutes before stretching. Make a gentle transition from the sedentary toward exercise with a short walk. Breathe slowly to calm yourself from stresses and to relax your muscles.

Myotatic or Stretch Reflex: Your Golgi organs, called proprioceptors--determine the stretch reflex. Move slowly into your stretch. Hold the stretch for 20 to 30 seconds until the muscle reflex unit relaxes, then ease down a bit more for the full muscle stretch. Work with the proprioceptors when stretching for increased muscle flexibility. This is a passive stretch; you relax all muscles.

You can also do active stretches. You contract one set of muscles, say the hamstrings by bringing your foot to your butt. Grasp your foot, and after 10 seconds of the active phase, gently pull the relaxed quads to their full length.

In yoga, stretches are held for minutes, and you might spend 20 minutes working and stretching one muscle group.

So, committing to stretching 3 times for 30 to 40 seconds for each of the main running muscle groups is not much of a hardship when you consider that it can keep you injury free and help you to run faster.

Alas, stretching is the third leading cause of running injuries! Slow muscle stretching, no bouncing, is the best way to avoid muscle strains. Repeat each stretch two or three times. Bouncing forces muscles past their natural range of motion, causing strains, and stimulates the anti-stretch reflex, which tears your individual muscle fibers. Mild muscle tension is your goal.

Protect your Achilles and Calf Muscles and Prevent Achilles Tendon Injuries.

Shortening of the Achilles tendon and the calf muscles puts extra pressure on them, and makes them more likely to strain. The Achilles is your largest tendon and very prone to inflammation and rupture. Pain and swelling anywhere from the heel up to where your calf muscles begin are hallmarks of Tendonitis. Add in stiffness upon wakening and pain upon running and you should see a specialist. Get treatment before you rupture the tendon or your recovery will be long.

Heel inserts help to reduce the strain on the Achilles tendon. Inserts are not effective unless you also work on the flexibility aspect with whichever two or three of the following stretches you prefer. Heel insert use is to some degree an admission that you are unwilling or unable to stretch the calf muscles!

Overpronation and other factors damage the Achilles tendon: a FULLY stretched pair of calf muscles, gastrocnemius and soleus, is your first line of defense against damage to the tendon, to the muscles, and to the all important muscle tendon unit. Stretch regularly to maintain your optimum flexibility.

Injuries are often due to imbalances. In addition to stretching the calf, do strengthening exercise for the shin muscles, which in runners, are often weak.

Stretching the calf muscles helps the rest of your leg muscles fall into place, and keeps your running biomechanics sound. Use these stretches to decrease Achilles Tendonitis and calf muscle strains. Appropriate length calf muscles reduce the pressure and the potential strain on the Achilles. The muscle tendon unit, where the muscle joins the tendon, is the most likely place to strain. Work with your muscle tendon unit...not against it.

The Calf Muscle is Two Muscles.

The gastrocnemius' muscle origin, or the attachment to connective tissue closest to the heart, is above the knee; the gastroc is best stretched with a straight knee. The soleus' muscle origin is below the knee, and can be stretched with a bent knee.

A/ The lunge (as in a sword fight) is suitable for both muscles. The gastric is stretched by keeping the heel of the back leg on the ground.

The front leg goes well forward--keep your balance and stay tall. In this upright position, lean forward until you feel the stretch in the straightened back leg.

During threshold pace training, many runners cruise through a warm-up, then pick up the pace. This is time efficient, and it's almost obligatory on hot or cold days, but do try at least one stretch. Stretching is best done with warm muscles, so find some shade on a hot day, or a wind sheltered spot on a cold day, and do this one all encompassing stretch.

The adapted lunge or the Leg Stretch.

Place one foot on a support which is 18 to 24 inches high. Adopt the lunge position, keeping the heel of the rear foot on the ground. Lean into the supported leg to stretch the buttock muscles, while experiencing a gentle pull on the Achilles tendon and soleus muscle. You'll also feel a pull on the quadriceps group of the supported leg. You should feel a gentle stretch on all posterior muscles of the rear leg, and on that Achilles. Arch your back to relax those muscles too. Repeat with the opposite foot on the support.

B/ Step Stretch. Stand with your toes on a step or stair with the heel extended over the edge. Drop the heels down slowly until you feel resistance in the muscle or tendon: hold for 20 seconds before pushing up (which is exercise). Do some with straight knees; do some with knees bent.

John Pagliano D.P.M. an injury expert for *Runner's World* suggests that people with high arches may want to give this exercise a miss because it can overstretch their Achilles complex. It can also overstretch the plantar fascia.

C/ Wall lean or the miss-named pushing the wall down. If you push, you're working the calf muscles--you should not work and stretch at the same time. With the step exercise, you have two distinct phases...work and stretch. With this next stretch, simply lean in toward the support.

Gastrocnemious Muscle--stand 3 to 4 feet from a wall, put your outstretched hands on the wall, shoulder width apart. Keep the knee straight and the heels flat on the ground. Lean in toward the wall slowly, keeping the body and knee straight: Stop when you think the calf is at its limit...when it and the Achilles tendons feel stretched.

D/ For the soleus muscle--as above but stand 2 to 3 feet away. Bend the knees until you feel the stretch. For both stretches, keep your heels on the ground by trying to press your heels into the surface.

E/ Ropes, pulleys, etc.

Place a piece of rope or karate belt under the sole of your foot, and then pull it toward you to give your calf muscle a stretch. As always, use a bent knee for the soleus muscle and straight knee for the gastrocnemius muscle. Some positions will also stretch your hamstrings, as will...

F/ Walking your fingers to your feet.

Start in the standing position with your feet facing forward, but about three feet apart. Hang your arms down and relax your back. Bend your knees as you place your hands on the floor in front of you...well in front of you. Straighten your legs; as you can see from the picture, locked knees are not essential. Now, walk your hands back toward your toes. Hold, relax per usual, and then get a little closer to your toes as you improve flexibility.

The very flexible person will be able to do this stretch with palms on the floor. Those of you with less muscle flexibility can walk back on the fingers until feeling the stretch in the hamstrings and calf muscles.

Whichever way you do page 75s stretch, keep your legs apart to help maintain balance. It also makes you feel better because your arms are closer to the ground, so your muscles appear to be more flexible. Don't put to much weight on your arms.

See also page 78s triangle stretch.

G/ At your desk or home, you can use one of the stretch gizmos on the market, or simply use a triangle of wood. Place your feet on the gismos at an appropriate angle several times per day to maintain or gain flexibility.

H/ Perhaps the simplest stretch. Any time you're standing round waiting, place one leg about six inches out in front of you. Keep most of your weight on the supporting leg; rest lightly on the heel of the leg to be stretched. Dorsi-flex the foot--use those little shin muscles to pull your toes up toward your shin. Hold for ten seconds and repeat. This exercise will also decrease your shin splint risk.

You can also place your toes a few inches up a wall or a step while keeping your heel on the ground to get a better stretch. If you are not too people conscious, lean forward and pull your toes toward you!

One of the best ways to stretch your calf muscles is to run on soft surfaces such as grass, mud and sand. These surfaces give, thus your heel sinks into the surface giving a nice stretch on each stride. You also have to work the calf more at push-off, which will make them stronger. Bring in soft surface running a bit at a time because you should not make sudden changes to your training. Warm up on grass.

When doing most of your hamstring stretches, you can also stretch the calf muscles. Hamstring muscle stretches with a straight leg are best--with a nearly locked knee. During your hamstring stretches, dorsi-flex the foot, bring the toes toward your shin, and you have two muscle groups stretched at one time.

Hamstrings--the back of the thigh.

A/ Sit on a soft surface, with your legs out in front of you. Keep the knees and back straight, and bend forward at the waist. Move your head down toward the knees.

B/ Barrier or hurdle stretch. Place your foot on a support at knee height or a little higher. Too high a support can lead to muscle tears. With a slightly bent knee to reduce the strain, ease your chest toward the knee. Keeping your back straight, roll around your hip joint rather than your vertebrae to get the stretch. Rise back up, and then repeat while also easing your vertebrae through their range of motion by moving forward to stretch out your back. Ready to advance? Press your knee down gently to make your leg straighter, which lengthens the hamstrings.

C/ Lie on your back, with your legs flat on the floor. Keep your hips pushed toward the center of the earth. With the right knee bent, bring it up toward your chest. You should feel no tightness because the hamstrings are relaxed. Keeping the right knee flexed at 90 degrees, grasp the calf area, and then slowly pull your lower leg up toward the sky as you straighten your leg. Stop when you feel tightness in the hamstring. Hold for 30 seconds, and do the other leg. A piece of rope, towel or a karate belt helps this and many other stretches. Place it under the ball of your foot and pull your straightened leg toward your head. Keep your hips and shoulders on the floor. You can also use a doorway and rest the heel of the leg to be stretched against the upper wall, while scooting your hip in to the base. The non-stretched leg rests on the floor through the doorway.

D/ Pick-ups. Eight-tenths of the way through half of your easy runs, do six 75-meter pick-ups at 5K pace. Your muscles will be warm, so relax, use good form, and feel the hamstrings and gluteals loosen up as you stride.

E/ Make like a triangle. Start on your haunches with your feet and hands about shoulder width apart and hands on the floor. Lift your knees up and raise your lovely butt toward the sky to straighten your legs. Your arms and back should be straight too so that you've formed a near perfect triangle with the ground as the base. Press the heels down to your comfort level for the Achilles and calf muscles. Bring your feet and hands closer together as dictated by the comfort of your hamstrings and back (and shoulder strength).

Gluteal or Hip Muscles: If these are tight, they resist movement on each stride and can cause knee problems. Gluteus maximus extends the femur. Its family stabilizes the hip.

Adopt an extended lunge position; allow the heel of the rear leg to come off the floor. Keep your hands on the floor, front knee well bent, with your knee close to or touching the chest. Feel the stretch in your butt. Do the barrier stretch, too.

Also, stand upright, or lie on a comfortable surface. Grasp one leg at the shin and pull the knee up toward your chest.

I-T band, or Ileotibial band--as above, but bring the left knee across the chest toward your right armpit, then re-stretch it toward the right side of your pelvis. Repeat for the other leg.

Another way to stretch the I-T band is the sideways lean while standing. Cross the left foot behind the right, but with your left foot close to your right. Keep your right hip still, but bend over to the right. Get an additional stretch by leaning the left hip away from your body and repeat with the other leg.

Or, start on your back. Flex the left knee and bring it up to your hip level. Place your right hand on the outside of the left knee and pull the knee over your right leg (which remains straight). Touch the floor with the inner part of your left knee. Roll your left arm out to the left to decrease the amount which you roll over. This also gives the hip flexors a stretch and is relaxing for your back. Do both legs.

To decrease knee injury risk, do straight leg raises, and develop your gluteus medius muscle with side lying, abduction leg raises with a straight leg. Do sets of 10 to 12.

Use the cable abduction device or elastic belts too. Abduct with a straight leg in sets of 15 to 20 with modest resistance.

Inner thigh. Sit on the floor with the soles of your feet together. Push your knees slowly toward the floor.

A tight piriformis (one of the butt muscles) can exacerbate runner's knee by rotating the knee. Stretch them by starting on your back with bent knees. Place the lateral side of your *left* foot on the right knee or thigh. Now pull your right thigh up toward your chest for 30 seconds. Then do the other leg.

Quadriceps: the four main muscles at the front of the leg are frequently the first to ache if mileage is increased, and as mentioned before, they also ache if you're not working your calf muscles enough. One of the quadriceps starts above the hip joint at the front and requires the body to be erect to stretch it. All four join to form the patella tendon inserting below the knee.

A/ On hands and knees like a dog, lift one leg back, then up, and pee...sorry, that was for a different book. Grasp the ankle and pull it toward your butt. Keep the knee bent (flexed) to stretch the front of the thigh.

B/ Stand upright, hold one foot and pull it up toward your bottom while keeping the knee pointed downwards. Get the bent knee even with your weight bearing knee if possible; keep your hips tucked inward. You can do this stretch in the prone position too, or seated on a chair with the leg that you are stretching dangling to the side.

Do not pull the bent leg out to the side because it'll put too much pressure on the knee. Holding the ankle with the opposite hand will decrease the tendency to poor form. Do not lean forward. Stand tall and flatten your back. Extend your hip backwards to accentuate the hip flexor stretch.

C/ Kneeling on a soft surface, slowly lean backwards. To get the full benefit, keep the area from the knee to shoulders in a line until your buttocks are resting on or near the ankles. Using the arms for support, stop at the point of resistance.

Straight leg raises while lying on your back are useful to strengthen the quads. Raise the leg 12 to 18 inches and hold for 10 to 15 seconds. Do a third of them with your toes pointed in and a third with them pointed out to work the outside and inside quad respectively.

Seated knee raises work the under publicized Ilio-soas group (the Iliacus and Psoas Major muscles). This pair helps to raise the thigh in fast running and hill work--that is, they flex the hip. Use the quad stretches which extend the hip joint to keep them loose.

Stretch the shin muscles too. While doing many of your quadriceps stretches, pull your toes gently to extend the ankle, which may decrease your risk of shin splints.

Back and Abdomen:

The trunk doesn't move much in running, but it needs to be flexible. Start by touching your toes each day for your lower back. With feet together or apart, knees bent or straight...bend over and ease your hands toward your feet. Just hang loose, let the tension go, and gently ease your spinal column through its range of motion: Don't force it.

Next. Stand with the feet apart, keeping the hips facing the front. Bend over to one side as far as possible...hold, and then repeat to the other side. Then, keeping the hips facing forward, rotate the top of your trunk to look behind...hold, swing slowly around to the front...then to the other side.

The lunge again--this time a relaxed position for the legs, then arch gently backwards to stretch each of those back and neck joints a bit.

You can also lie on your stomach, go into a banana shape by raising the head and shoulders, plus bring the feet and legs off the surface. This stretches the abdominals while exercising the back muscles. Experts call this an active spinal extension. Push up with your hands if the emphasis is on the stretch.

To counteract the tightening of your hip flexors from hours of sitting in a chair...stand up every hour to arch your back and stretch the hip flexors and abdominals.

Protect your back by keeping the abdominal muscles strong, which helps you to run tall, and decrease injuries. Don't let your running's weakest link be a supporting muscle group.

Lower Back and Shoulder Stretch:

Stand about 3 feet from a sturdy support with your weight evenly balanced on the soles and heels. Bend at the waist and place both hands on the support shoulder-width apart. This means flexing your hips to make a table platform with your back. Your hands should be higher than your back so that you can push your shoulders down for the stretch. You'll be bent over enough at the hips to stretch your hamstrings too.

Then, stand nose to wall with your right arm horizontal. Slowly turn your upper torso to face the left and feel the stretch in the front of the right shoulder.

Next, adopt a sitting position. Raise your right arm to the horizontal with the elbow bent behind your neck. Grasp the elbow with your left hand and pull the elbow round so that your right hand goes round your left shoulder.

Done the banana stretch? Roll onto your back. Place your feet under your knees and shoulder width apart. Roll your hips off the ground and arch your back, raising your butt up to stretch your back and hip extensors.

Make stretching a habit.

Decrease general aches from properly exercised muscles by stretching pre and post running. You'll maintain flexibility, allowing a full range of movement, and reduce injury risk.

Be pedestrian. Stretch slowly without bouncing to avoid the myotatic reflex, which leads to micro muscle fiber tears. Hold stretches for 30 seconds and repeat three times.

Regular stretching, using ice or cold water (see Chapter Five's tips), just after training, and avoiding sudden changes to your training, will decrease your experiences with Delayed Onset Muscle Soreness (DOMS).

Little muscle fiber tears need rest or you'll injure yourself. Run too fast or do too many Saturday intervals, and your Sunday run's biomechanics will suffer due to fatigue: You'll come up achy and lame by Monday or Tuesday. Build up your quality running by adding 400 meters at a time to develop your muscle's resistance to fatigue, and their resistance to breaking down.

DOMS peaks at 48 hours after quality training. You can work with Yakovlev's principle (page 46) by training moderately hard on back to back days. The second session is done before the peak of soreness from session one. Running 40 miles per week? Two x 2 miles at 15K pace is a breeze, and you should be able to run 12 x 400 meters at 5K pace the next day. Stay relaxed for both sessions, and then rest, including a long run before doing your next quality session. Add 400 meters per month and reach back to back sessions of 3 x 2-miles followed by 16 x 400 meters.

Hydrate and feed your muscles to keep them well lubricated for a happy, injury free life.

Chapter Seven

Step 2 of Half-Marathon Training

ANAEROBIC THRESHOLD

In Steps Two & Three of Half-Marathon Training you merely convert your fartlek sessions to more formalized training to maximize your anaerobic threshold, then your VO2 maximum. You will spend 8 to 10 weeks at each step. Racing 10K to 10 miles half-way through each 10 weeks will set you up for half-marathons at the end of each step.

According to Jeff Galloway, "Hill repeats, Anaerobic threshold sessions, and or VO2 max intervals at 5K to 2 mile race pace...provide the edge to any runner who is trying to push beyond thresholds of current performance."

Running faster half-marathon race times is achieved by a gradual increase in training load by:

* Improving the quality for some of your miles.
* Or with increased mileage.

Step Two is almost the last chance to add mileage for your aerobic base. Two extra runs of four to six miles, for instance, will take months to show up as an improvement in your aerobic endurance. Add them in the same week and they'll only take a few weeks to show up as injuries! It's better to add a 3 to 4 mile run for 2 weeks, then increase it to 5 miles for another two weeks. Later, push it to 6 miles before adding weight training for the rest of your life!

If the last couple of months were your first experience of running 40 to 45 miles per week, don't add mileage for the rest of this year. Your long run has reached it peak. It will take the 20 weeks of Step Two & Three for your muscles to fully adapt to doing 15 to 18 mile runs on a regular basis.

Stay hydrated on those long runs, and consume a little carbohydrate on the fly. Carbo on the run maintains your brains sugar level, which may maintain your dopamine level, which boosts your coordination, running energy, mood and concentration. You'll handle the physical fatigue better, and your running muscles also appreciate the sugar.

200 calories per hour (32 ounces of a typical sports drink or 13 ounces of apple juice plus 20 ounces of water to make it a 5 to 6 percent solution). The juice gives you less weight to carry, or you can use a couple of gel packs plus water.

In addition to long runs, do Chapter 9 and 10s cross training.

* Start with 5 miles, and build to a 20-mile bike ride once or twice a week at gentle effort.
* In addition, start with 10 minutes and build to 40 minutes of weight training twice a week.

These short sessions help to balance your muscle build-up, correcting many weaknesses which can develop from a run only program. Biking stretches and relaxes the hamstrings and helps your hill running. Weight training makes you work your upper body and trunk muscles. These sessions also lay the foundation for 20 mile race training.

Step Two for the Half-Marathon.

ANAEROBIC THRESHOLD PACE RUNNING for SPEED ENDURANCE.

Tempo Runs & Cruise Intervals at 15K to 10 mile pace.

Many coaches don't consider threshold pace to be speedwork. In my book (literally and philosophically) any time you run faster than race pace you are speed training. Use threshold training wisely and it will make you stronger and better able to handle half-marathon race pace.

Tempo or anaerobic threshold running teaches more of your muscle cells to work efficiently for long periods, allowing you to run farther at a fast pace. You'll train at or slightly faster than half-marathon race pace for one to four miles at a time, take a rest, then run the same or a shorter distance again. You should run at 80 to 92 percent of your maximum heartrate (HR). The pace should be only a slight challenge to maintain.

You've been doing this training for about 30 weeks. Those fartlek sessions with long reps were at anaerobic threshold!

Your build up of base running at 60-80 % of maximum HR, plus strides, fartlek and hills, and practice races have set you up for more formal sessions at anaerobic threshold.

Bring in these anaerobic threshold runs gently. Early sessions will be barely over 80 percent max heartrate--long intervals of about a mile with a short breather...more for a mental than a physical recovery. You'll need to think about form on these reps. You will run comfortably hard, but not all out for these sessions. As with those fartlek sessions, run about 10 percent of your monthly miles at threshold pace.

Start with about three repeats of half a mile to one mile if you're here for the first time. Keep these sessions short enough and slow enough that you can maintain your hill session at 5K effort about three days later.

After a few weeks of running these threshold sessions, you'll be able to increase running pace toward 90 percent of your maximum heartrate. Many physiologists recommend 90 percent as the top range for cruising through these sessions. Most of these runs will be at 15K or 10-mile race pace to hit that pulse target. When you're tired two days after your long run, or when the weather is bad, it may be half-marathon pace: It will rarely be slower. If your heartrate is 90 percent at your half-marathon pace, you should add rest to the next few days because you may be overtrained. Achy quads, or a higher than usual resting heartrate on awakening are reliable signs of overtraining.

As researcher, coach and author, Jack Daniels Ph.D. says, "Anaerobic Threshold is the pace or intensity beyond which blood lactate concentration increases dramatically due to your body's inability to supply all its oxygen needs. As you get fitter, your red line rises from 80 % of maximum HR to 90-95 percent." You should be at 15K pace; 10K pace puts most of us over the red line because it is too harsh.

Some coaches call this aerobic threshold training, because you're pushing up the pace at which you can run using predominantly aerobic pathways for energy. You're increasing the speed which you can run before you go into oxygen debt. Your goal is to run close to your maximum oxygen uptake level without the build up of lactic acid.

Tempo or threshold running is also the pace that you can sustain for close to an hour, which will be:

* Half-marathon pace for elite runners;
* 15K or 10 mile pace for middle of the pack club runners;
* 10K pace for most recreational runners.

Use the percentage of your maximum heartrate to determine your threshold training pace. But, consider the running speed of a 50 to 60 minute race as your back-up training pace.

Tempo runs require you to respect heat. High temperature and high humidity combined = danger.

		80	*85*	*90*	*95*	*100... real temperature*
		Equivalent Temperature (Fahrenheit)				
Rela-	*40*	79	86	93	101	110
tive	*50*	81	88	96	107	*120*
	60	82	90	100	*114*	*132*
humi-	*70*	85	93	106	*124*	*144*
dity	*80*	86	97	*113*	*136*	Death Valley
(%)	*90*	88	102	*122*	Death Valley (but wet)	

Got a long threshold pace session or race at high temperature and high humidity? Run a couple hours later. Stay hydrated and stay out of the sun when possible. Slow down, and pace yourself on heartrate goals instead of speed goals.

The speed table for threshold pace is on pages 202-203.

Note: Grass and Dirt trails are great surfaces for training at 15K pace. See page 153.

Continuous Tempo Runs, or Sustained Runs.

After a few sessions of cruise intervals, you can run continuous tempo pace for 4 to 5 miles. Run them at half-marathon goal pace or 80 percent of max HR the first couple of times, then ease the pace down to 15K speed. Or is it up to 15K speed? Later, alternate the sustained or continuous tempo runs with intervals at threshold pace.

You'll be training for at least 8 weeks in Step Two, using 8 to 10 sessions at threshold pace. When increasing your quality running you have two options:

* Substitute threshold pace running for the relaxed fartlek session one week;
* Then, exchange threshold pace for your hill running the next week.
* More competitive runners will add this threshold pace running to their original two speed sessions.

This gives you four quality runs each week. Although long runs are at easy pace, their length makes them quality training days. If you do add this third speed session, refer to the stretching in Chapter Six to avoid tightening up.

In Chapter Three, you were asked to run 4 to 6 miles of your medium length run at close to 80 percent of your max HR. If you bump up the running pace by 15 seconds or so, you should be at or above 80 percent. Split this 4 to 6 miles into mile repeats at another 10 seconds per mile faster, and you've got yourself cruise intervals at 85-90 percent of max HR, or 10 mile race pace.

You could run all of your threshold training at half-marathon pace, about 80 percent of your maximum heartrate, but your threshold is more stimulated by running at 15K pace. It's only 15 to 20 seconds per mile slower than 10K pace and will:

* Make you more efficient at running the faster pace...you will need less oxygen and sugar per mile.
* Raise your speed endurance as you develop better coordination of muscle contractions during repetitions.
* Raise the point or threshold (or increases the running speed) at which huge amounts of lactic acid is produced.
* Increase your body's ability to absorb excess lactic acid.

Net effect--you can run more relaxed at half-marathon pace.

An additional side affect of threshold pace running is that you improve your VO2 Maximum! Psychologically, it's nice to run 10 to 15 seconds faster than half-marathon pace.

Lower mileage runners can adjust the following sessions down to 10 % of weekly mileage: high mileage runners can try this four week rotation while racing once a month.

Two times 3 miles at half-marathon pace, which should be 80 percent of your maximum heartrate.

3 x 2 miles at 15K pace...true threshold pace.

4 x 2,000 meters at 15K pace with very short rests.

5 x one mile at 10K pace...faster than threshold for most, but it will help your buffering system. Finish with 4 x 400 meters at 5K pace, as preparation for Step Three of your half-marathon training.

The constant is the recovery. Take a 400 rest for all sessions except the 400s, when one minute will suffice.

Run a variety of sessions to maintain your interest. Keep the recoveries short to ensure that you give your muscles a chance to educate themselves! Match each threshold pace session with some kind of speed at short distances:

Run your hills or resistance training and fartlek sessions using short efforts of one to two minutes.

Retain your long runs of course. The long run is the cement which holds your training blocks together.

Your weekly training will progress something like this:

	Day One	Two	Three	Four	
Probably	*Sat*	*Sun*	*Tues*	*Thurs*	
	Hill repeats (in meters)	Long run	Fartlek	Anaerobic Threshold	Total Miles
Wk 1	12 x 400H	17	8 / 5.0F	T5	45
2	8 x 600H	18	24 / 4.0F	CI5	45
3	20 x 200H	18	8 / 5.0F	T4	44
4	12 x 300	13	20 / 3.0F	CI3	35

Race a 10K, run an easy 10 on Monday and a gentle fartlek session on Wednesday, and then repeat the first four weeks.

H and F stand for hills and fartlek respectively.
T5 is a 5-mile tempo run at half-marathon pace with a 3-mile warm-up and cooldown at one minute per mile slower.
CI5 means 5 miles of cruise intervals at about 15K race pace, but with only a short recovery between reps. Because two of the fartlek sessions are still long efforts, you'll have 6 threshold pace sessions per month. As with Chapter Three, those 300s the week pre-race are on the flat.

The designation Day One to Day Four does not mean that you train hard 4 days in a row. It's up to you which days of the week are running days. Saturday, Sunday, Tuesday and Thursdays work for many 4 day a week runners, with active rest or cross training on Monday and Wednesdays, and total rest on Fridays.

Most runners prefer to train moderately hard only twice a week, and will switch a few sessions around (page 90). You'll get four threshold pace sessions per month, and two hill sessions. The closer those middle miles on day 4 are to 80 percent of max HR, the harder you will be training!

	Day One	Two	Three	Four	Total
1	H 12 x 400	17	T5	12	45
2	F 32 / 4.0	18	CI5	12	45
3	H 20 x 200	18	T4	10	44
4	12 x 300	13	CI3	8	35

Anaerobic threshold training, if practiced for a long enough period, should allow you to race the half-marathon 5 seconds per mile faster than after Step One. Set your goal pace at 25 seconds per mile slower than your current 10K race pace, then if you feel good at 10 miles, increase pace by a few seconds per mile for a strong finish.

Six to ten sessions of cruising at 15K or 10 mile pace bring huge fitness rewards. Then maintain those gains while working at the final aspect of your half-marathon running.

Try to arrange your 10-week phase at anaerobic threshold to culminate in a second half-marathon race. Your last week pre race will be really easy, and similar to week four above, but with only 10 or 11 miles on Day two and a five mile run on Day Four.

Note: The usual advice on windy days is to run into the wind on the way out, so that if you feel bad, you'll be pushed back home on the return. Another option is to run with the wind on the way out and enjoy the cooling affect of running into the wind on the way back. This is best used on hot days, especially for tempo runs. For chilly days, it is probably best to have the easy running in the second half of the run.

Doing cruise Intervals on a 400-meter track? Four laps is about 9 meters short of one mile, so multiply your 1,600 time (in seconds) by 1.0058 to get the mile equivalent, or about 2 extra seconds for that pesky 9 meters. A 5-minute 1,600 equals a 5.01.74. A 7-minute 1,600 equals a 7.02.36 mile.

Long rests during threshold training defeat your purpose.

How much of your training is likely to be at ideal anaerobic HR while running 1,200s with short rests. This particular athlete ran 6 x 1,200 meters on a nearly straight section of grass with no undulations. Using a two-minute rest, (200 meters of mostly jogging...HR down to 120) he averaged 4.37 per repeat (slowest was first at 4.40; fastest 4.35 in the middle and a 4.39 finish). His max HR is 180; a seasoned runner of several decades, his goal HR for 15K pace is 162 or 90 % of max.

Repeat #	1	2	3	4	5	6
Point at which HR reached 162	900	550	350	250	200	150
HR at 400	149	157	162	163	164	163
HR at 800	159	163	164	163	162	162
HR at 1,200	163	164	164	164	163	163
Percentage of time heart is at 15K intensity	25	54	62	80	83	87

Note: He ran the entire 4.5 miles at 15K pace!

* The highest HR this day was 165, which would be 10K intensity, and not the goal of his session. He was at 165 for only a few seconds because the athlete reduced pace.
* The relatively slow first repeat contributed to only 25 percent of it being at 15K HR goals. However, all 1200s were at his 15K speed for the year, and the sensible start set up a pleasurable session.
* His 85 % HR of 153 was passed well before the 400 meter point in all remaining repeats. Although the 90 % level took 550 meters for the second repeat, he had 54 % of his repetition at goal HR, and over three-quarters was above 85 % max HR.
* As the session progressed, a pleasant amount of fatigue set in and 90 % of max HR was achieved early in each

rep, giving him 83 % of his time, or eleven and a quarter minutes at his 15K goal HR during the last three repeats.

* While he had the legs to do at least one more repeat, he saved himself for his long run the next day.
* He eased the pace just a little for the last two repeats to stop himself hitting 10K HR intensity.

How can we improve his anaerobic threshold?

1. Have him run another 4.5 mile threshold session every 4 to 5 days for 6 to 8 weeks.
2. Match each threshold session with fartlek or 5K pace running, alternating with hills.
3. Include tempo runs and longer repeats. When he does this session again, consider:
4. Running the first rep a bit faster and taking a one minute rest before the second repeat, which should get him to a 162 HR by perhaps 600 and 400 meters during those repeats, resulting in an additional 450 meters at a HR of 162. Then use 2 minute rests so that:
5. He can add an additional repeat every 6 months to reach 6 miles at speed. Or,
6. Increase the length of repeats to one mile, which would give him an additional 92 seconds at his threshold HR on all six repeats. This would take his current 47 % at goal HR during the first three repeats to 62 %. In total, he would get an additional 1.5 miles or over 9 minutes at goal HR.
7. Ask him to do a maximum HR test (fast uphill 200 to 300 meters) to make sure his max HR has not dropped to 178. If his max HR is 178, the training time at 164 HR would be in his 10K range. While that would be a very nice Chapter Eleven session, unless he can race 15K at this intensity, it is too harsh for anaerobic threshold training. (Note: If he is training in his 10K range, he will obviously not be able to race a 15K at that pace!)

Chapter Eight

Half Marathon Step 3

INTERVAL TRAINING at 5K to 2 MILE RACE PACE (VO2 MAXIMUM PACE)

Maximum Oxygen Uptake Capacity, the amount of oxygen which you can absorb while running, in combination with how economically you run dictates how fast you can run a certain distance. Interval training at 5K to 2 mile race pace, which is 95 to 100 percent of your current VO2 max, (and 95 to 98 percent of your max heartrate), will improve your maximum oxygen uptake, plus your running efficiency.

The combination of more oxygen into your body and greater running efficiency will allow you run faster for the same amount of energy or effort. You will not work any harder in your next half-marathon, but every 1,000 calories you burn will take you a greater distance. You'll race faster.

To paraphrase this author's favorite article on running, from an ancient *Scientific American*, "Interval training shifts your metabolic equilibrium (enzyme actions etc,) so that you can run aerobically at a higher speed than you used to," hence, you'll be able to race faster.

Intervals are still a dirty word to some, but dirt does not matter: you've been running intervals for several months already. Your short fartlek efforts at 5K intensity and hill repeats are interval sessions at close to VO2 max. During this phase though, you will do more formal sessions with a watch and perhaps a track to encourage rapid movement.

Numerous studies show that running short distances at good speed is the best way to improve running form and efficient use of oxygen. Interval training should not hurt you. You can do anything from a few strides to 24 times a quarter mile...you get the same benefits:

* Smoother running...which reduces injury risk...and you
* Absorb more oxygen, yet conserve your oxygen and energy.
* Further improve your heart as a muscular pump.
* Further stimulation of mitochondria and red blood cells.
* You race faster at a given effort...with very few sessions.
* Intervals are precise: you can measure your progress.

By-passed 10K racing? Your 5K running speed for interval training at VO2 max should be 2 to 3 seconds per 400 meters faster than your recent 10K race pace. When training at 2 mile pace, use 4-5 seconds per lap faster than 10K pace, or 2 seconds per lap faster than 5K pace.

Interval training will get your muscles used to running fast for a long (overall) period of time. Intervals allow you to do huge volumes at a fast training pace...without wearing yourself out. Achieve the target speed, and then emphasize improving endurance at that speed. Add about half a mile of reps each time you do a particular session.

Interval Training Basics.

Running track intervals for the first time? Run a warm-up and stretch. Flexibility determines your range of movement, your potential stride length. As you've read before, muscles are longer when warmed up; they work better when they are long, exerting the same amount of force with less effort.

Now then, don't jump straight into long sessions of intervals. Feel as comfortable for the last repeat as you do for the first repeat. Run the last few reps as fast as the early ones. But don't make the last few reps significantly faster.

Don't feel wasted afterwards. Feel as if you could run another interval or two when you've completed the session.

Relax your way through these interval sessions. You're running much slower than maximum speed, so work on a relaxed and economical running motion.

At 100 percent physical effort, your muscles tense up. For every set of muscles which is working, there is a group which is relaxing back for its next contraction. Relax and run smoothly during these sessions to increase your running velocity or your speed at 95 percent of your VO2 max. It will lead to faster races.

Start with 5K pace intervals.

Beginners progression.

* Week one--Bends & straights--stride quite fast along the straight then jog the bends. Run 8 to 12 laps to give 16 to 24 striders to improve your running form and get your muscles used to the track surface.

* Week two--16 x 200 meters with a 200 rest.

* Week three--10 x 300 meters. A little slower speed than the 200s and take a 300 recovery. Run two straights and one bend for the repetition, and two bends and a straight for the recovery. Use lane 4 or 5. This reduces the strain on your ankles to hips—there's a tendency to lean into the curve.

* Week four--8 x 200 and 4 x 400 meters. You'll need to run economically in the 400s in order for you to keep going for the extra 100 meters at the pace of your 300s.

Training pace should be no faster than your 2-mile race speed, which is 100 percent of your VO2 maximum. Two mile pace is about 10 to 12 seconds per mile faster than the speed of your best recent 5,000 meters. Sessions at this modest pace give your leg muscles a chance at adjusting to the track surface. However, 5K pace is better than 2 mile pace your first time through this schedule. Your goal is to avoid hurting during these sessions.

Use the sprinters start point when running in the middle lanes. Your start point for a 400-meter effort is about one third of the way through the first curve. If you ran a whole lap in lane five, starting and finishing at the same spot, you add 26.8 meters per lap if the lanes are the standard 42 inches wide. That's about 5.4 seconds for the 80 seconds per 400-meter runner.

* Week five--10 x 300 again. Pace judgment should improve with practice; aim to run your reps at even pace. Many runners blitz the first hundred then stagger through the last part of each rep. Comfortable interval sessions require even pace for the individual reps, and even pace for all 10 reps. If you run more than 50 miles per week, build toward twenty reps and then decrease the rest interval.

* Week six--6 x 200 and 6 x 400 meters with the same jog recovery. Keep the session easy by running at 5K pace. Maintain good form for the entire lap...assess your running form every 100 meters. 400s have the advantage that you start and finish each effort at the same place in lane one.

* Week seven--4 x 300, and 3-4 x 600 meters.

* Week eight--6 x 200, and 8 x 400 meters.

Then alternate sessions using mostly short reps at 2 mile pace, with sessions of longer reps at 5K race pace.

Experienced interval runners can try this nine-session progression:

* 12 times 300 meters at two mile pace with 200 rests.

* 10 x 400 meters at 5K pace with 200 rests.

* 8 x 600 meters at 5K pace with 400 rests.

* 15 x 300 at two mile pace.

* 10 x 400 ONE second per rep faster than 5K pace.

* 10 x 600 at 5K pace.
* Either 18 x 300 at two mile pace or 15 x 300 at 5K pace with very short rests.
* 10 x 400 at two mile pace (2 seconds a lap faster than 5K pace).
* 12 x 600 at 5K pace.

Note how each distance progresses in a different way. Gershler, the great German coach who described five variables to adjust interval sessions, would be proud of us. The speed of the 400s increase; the number of 300 reps rises, before the recovery is shortened; and, the quantity of 600s increases. Once you are satisfied with the number of repeats, or the volume of training at close to VO2 max, decrease the recoveries toward 60 seconds or less. A 200-meter restive jog is the ideal after each 600-meter rep.

By stimulating your energy systems over a series of interval sessions, more of each rep will become aerobic. You'll go into oxygen debt at 400 meters into a 600-meter effort instead of at 200. You will be anaerobic for less of each rep: You will be able to race faster.

One Olympian wrote an article advocating 400 meter repeats for a runner who starts races fast and finishes slow; he also advised 400s for someone who runs slowly in the middle of races. What these runners probably needed was to start the race at appropriate pace for them, instead of running too fast at the start. Avoid running 400s week in, week out. The 600s keep you in the training zone for a higher percentage of your total speed session. Don't miss their benefits. And build up the total number of repeats which you run to improve your endurance.

Maintain those long runs of course or you'll have a tendency to start fast because of your legspeed, but you will not have the stamina to maintain pace. The half marathon is truly an endurance event.

Despite months of prior training, including those fartlek sessions at 5K pace, your progress will be phenomenal for several sessions. Be prepared for progress to slow as your running form and efficiency is perfected, as you get close to your potential--the potential at your current training level.

Keep the speed of reps in the proper relationship to your race pace. Taking a break from half-marathon training to race a couple of mile events? 200s at mile speed is useful.

However, running 300s at 3,000 meters (or two mile) pace is better for half-marathon preparation; do 400s at 5,000 meters pace. Gradually increase the speed of 400s to run 3,000 meter or 2 mile pace. Aim toward 6,000 meters per interval session. You only need a small amount of running at 2-mile race pace to maximize your oxygen assimilation ability. Save your legs by running most of your intervals at 5K pace.

Running longer intervals at VO2 max

further stimulates your VO2 maximum and running economy. You'll run a greater proportion of your intervals in oxygen debt, stimulating more adaptation to your heart and running muscles. You'll have to think about running form.

Mile repeats and 1,000s at 5K pace are great sessions. Three miles of long repeats is a time efficient training session if you keep recoveries to three minutes. Rotate:

3 x one mile with 400 meters rest;

5 x 1,000 meters with 200 rests;

One mile; then 2 x 1,000; then one mile.

Running 3 to 5 of these sessions augments your peaking. Or just use one of these sessions the weekend before each race. Eventually, you'll want to run 4 to 5 miles of reps.

Like to Run Fast Twice a Week?

You'll get four VO2 max sessions per month. Rotate hills, fartlek and anaerobic threshold pace sessions on day one.

The two long runs each week are crucial to half-marathon success. V4 means 4 miles of intervals at 5K to 2-mile pace. Rotate 300s to 600s. Other abbreviations are the same as on prior pages. As usual, race a 10K after your 35-mile week!

	Day One	Two	Three	Four	Total
1	H 12 x 400	17	V4	12	45
2	F 15/4	18	V4	12	45
3	T4	18	V4	10	44
4	12 x 300	14	CI3	8	35

Running fast three times per week? That is, you run part of your 12 mile run at 80 to 90 percent max HR. You will still only do four VO2 max sessions per month, but you'll also get three hill sessions each month instead of only one. You also retain your slew of threshold pace runs.

1	H 12 x 400	17	V4	T5	45
2	H 8 x 600	18	V4	CI5	45
3	H 20 x 200	18	V4	T4	44
4	V3	14	F 3.0	CI3	35.5

5 Race a 10K, run a fifteen the next day, then run a mid-week hilly fartlek session and repeat the first four weeks. The speed table for Intervals is on pages 204-205.

Intervals at 5K pace is a great chance to experiment with your stride length and knee lift. How much harder or easier is it to run at a certain pace with high knees verses a shorter, more rapid stride? A half-inch too high on each stride costs 10 percent of your energy. Calves should propel you forward, not upward for speed and for low ground impact.

Don't overstride.

If your foot is still traveling forward when it hits the ground, the heel acts as a break, causing stress and damage on every stride. Impact stresses may show up as sore knees, shin splints, a tender back, or simply with slow running because you've set up a breaking action on every stride.

Rest up to race the Half-Marathon more seriously. Rest up a bit every 4 to 5 weeks for a serious 10K to 10 mile race. You can also race at the 5K most months, but due to tired muscles aim for 20 seconds slower than your best.

After 10 to 20 weeks of Intervals though, you'll test yourself at the half-marathon. Rest up from your training:

Mileage: Reduce your overall mileage by 20-50 percent over 5 to 15 days. You do less each day as you get closer to the half-marathon. Easy runs in the penultimate week would be 6s instead of 8s. Cut one or two completely if you're a seventy miles per week person. The long runs can be 14 and 11 for the two weekends pre-race instead of the usual 18. Cut a couple miles off that midweek long run too. If your usual week is 70 miles, try 55 and 40 miles pre-race.

Not convinced there are benefits to resting up and healing months of muscle tissue trauma. Try this: weight train the day after an 8 mile run and note how easy it feels. Three or 4 days later, do your weight session the day after your 18-mile run. Long runs and hard training depletes muscle power. The second weight session will feel much harder. In fact, it's easy to strain muscles on this day. Resting with long tapers improves your racing speed. The goal is to recover from your weeks of training without de-conditioning. And don't weight train just before a race.

The speedwork...Lets say you do 5 miles at speed every three to four days. A gradual reduction over your last five sessions might look like this.

One. A 5-mile tempo run--this is 20 days pre-race, too early to rest up. It could be a low-key 10K race, which you run within 10 seconds per mile of your best recent time. It would still feel hard, but not too taxing.

Two. VO2 max at 2 mile pace. 300 or 400-meter efforts. It's 16 days to the race, so you can do your normal amount...but don't increase pace or the number of reps. This session consolidates your training from previous weeks. You will have run two miles less than usual the day before.

Three. A different VO2 max session. Long reps at 5K pace. This is a crucial session. Long reps at VO2 max keep you close to your VO2 max for a greater percentage of your running time than short reps. Used to 6-7 times 1,200 meters? Try 5 times 1,000 meters. This is significantly less than usual, plus you have the speed from four days ago, and you know that you have the strength. As Olympic Gold medalist, Steve Ovett's coach, the late Harry Wilson said "practice running relaxed at 5K pace with less effort."

Four. Much less than usual...it's 8 days to race day. Long reps again. Cruise 3 x one mile at 15K pace. It will be easy because you've decreased mileage. You're used to running 5 to 6 reps at this pace. Resist the temptation to run 10K pace. 15K pace is much faster than half marathon pace, and you get the full benefit from threshold training at 15K pace: Save your legs for next weeks big race.

Five. Two miles at speed. 800 at 5K pace, 5 times 300 at two mile pace, 800 at 5K should suffice. A good taper can improve your running economy by 6 percent.

Week by week tapers are shown in Chapters 12 through 14. Generally, you also taper for-half marathon racing with: Less mileage, but train at the same intensity for a small amount of your mileage. Rest in all spheres of your life. Penultimate week...do 80 percent of your normal mileage. Final week...do 50 to 60 percent. Don't go for "personal training records" in any session. Don't do any hill reps in the last 10 days.

Racing your Half-marathon:

Be patient. Run the first mile of the race at controlled pace. Don't waste energy weaving in and out of people in the first mile. Gaps will open up in due course. Then, ease around the obstacle or settle behind someone running appropriate pace for you. Groups form by the end of the first mile, so you can help each other to about halfway. Some runners will drop off the pace, while others pick the pace up by two or three seconds per mile for negative splits. It depends on how well you pace that first mile as to which group of runners you belong.

Practice negative splits in your 5K and 10Ks. Start 5 seconds per mile slower than even pace, and then speed up to race pace for the middle third of the race: finish the last third at 5 seconds per mile faster than average pace. Use a 10 to 15 seconds per mile difference in long training runs.

Keep your running smooth; you didn't do all those long runs, anaerobic threshold miles and VO2 max sessions just to raise your threshold and VO2 max limit...they taught you economical running for mile after mile. Think about your form for a minute during every mile of the race.

At some stage you will hurt. Don't slow down. If you're running at appropriate pace, you should focus on your running form. See pages 39 & 42, drop your arms low for a few strides, then gradually bring them up just high enough to keep your stride rapid and smooth. Feel tired? Look up and speed up by 5 seconds per mile for a half mile. Maintain speed around corners and speed up by a fraction 100 meters before the top of hills, then stride downhill.

After you've worked through the three steps of half-marathon training once, and raced several Halfs, you can run all types of training each month. You could follow any of the schedules in Chapters 12 to 14 based on a combination of mileage and the number of times that you like to run quality; or make your own schedule.

For example, during each 3 to 5 week loop through the schedule you can do all sessions once. The number of rest days you take will dictate whether you have a 21 or 35 or perhaps a 28 day rotation.

The basic running rules are unchanged: Alternate long intervals with short intervals; Do one in four sessions against resistance...hills or sand.

For 10 percent of your monthly training miles.
Anaerobic or Lactate Threshold Training. At threshold pace, alternate continuous tempo runs with cruise intervals.

6 miles at half-marathon pace...80 to 85 % of max HR;

4 miles at 15K or 10 mile pace...true threshold tempo speed at 85-90 percent of max HR;

One and a half mile repeats, do three or more. About 90 percent max HR if it feels right;

Mile reps at your red line...cruise in control; with practice, your muscles will accumulate less lactic acid.

For another 10 percent of your training miles.

VO2 max pace--2 mile to 5K pace:

300s to 600s and relaxed fartlek at the same speed. Alternate short reps with long ones at 5K pace. Take short rests to stop yourself from sprinting. Do mile repeats too.

For five percent of your miles, do hill or resistance training sessions. Do one session of short reps for knee lift and one of long reps for strength endurance. Work with the hills; don't fight them by running too hard.

And Long Runs. Up to 18 miles, or one third of your average weekly mileage, but don't run for more than 3 hours. Run at 65 to 70 percent max HR. Add a mile each time through the 21 to 35 day half-marathon schedule.

Many runners make the mistake of tapering for their longest run. Run 3 to 5 miles at 5K pace to fatigue your fast twitch fibers the day before a long run and you'll increase the training benefit of your long run. You don't need fresh legs to run at easy pace--even for 18 miles The combination of faster than race pace, followed by slower than half marathon pace running increases the effect of your training.

Can you bounce back from speed sessions rapidly? No, then they're too hard for you currently. See pages 45 to 69.

Interval training places more mental strain on you as concentrate on running form at high speed for 2 minutes or more. Intervals also put you under more physical strain than you were used to during fartlek or anaerobic threshold sessions. Think of yourself as being powerful and energetic during intervals. Imagine your favorite strong animals, and provided you do your interval training at 5K pace or just a few seconds per mile faster, you'll feel like a strong animal.

The Future: Improving your half-marathon time

requires a gradual increase in training load. Increase:

* The number of miles which you run each month;
* The resistance you experience for some of those miles;
* And the speed at which you run some of those miles.

When moving up from 50 to 60 miles per week you can:

* Run 5 % upgrades for hill repeats instead of 3 %;
* Do hill repeats with wet shoes or in mud and sand;
* Try some hills at 2 mile intensity instead of 5K effort;
* Run more of your anaerobic threshold at 15K pace instead of half-marathon pace;
* Speed through some of your VO2 max sessions at 2 mile pace instead of 5K pace;
* Stride through very long repeats at 5K and then 2 mile pace instead of short reps.

Change one factor at a time, or a little bit of two factors. Example: In the week that you add a 5 mile run to increase mileage, you could run two reps up a steeper hill in your hill session; or you could run a one mile effort at 5K pace in the middle of 16 x 400 instead of doing 20 x 400.

A track experiment: When running 400 meter repeats at 5K pace or a bit faster, a person with a maximum exercise HR of 175 can take over 200 meters to get to his 10K training HR (161) and only reach his 5K HR of 166 for the last 40 to 50 meters of each Interval. Here are the HR splits at each 100 for an 80 second 400 meters. 148, 159, 164, 167.

Despite running slightly faster than 5K pace, so gaining very good skills at economical running, his heart was only at *5K intensity for about 10 percent of his Interval training.*

Now, what happens if our hero slows down to 5K pace, but runs 800s?

Distance	HR	HR
200	159	157
400	164	163
600	169	169
800	171	167
Finish time	2.50	2.53

Yes my friends, that 167 HR at the end of the second repeat was a reflection of our runner slowing down. Observe:

* Slightly lower HR at 400 meters secondary to slower running (compared to his earlier 400s).
* But, he was only seconds away from hitting his 5K HR goal of 166 at the end of the first lap, and spent well over 300 meters above 166, or about *40 percent of his Interval training at his 5K HR goal.*
* If he took shorter recoveries, he could reach his 166 HR goal earlier in each repeat, though this would make the session feel and of course be harsher. Hate the author please, because your goal is to reduce rest periods to spend over 50 % of the time at 95 % of your max HR.

We know that long repeats keep you in your training zone for a greater percentage of your training time. Lets see how much more time he will spend in his training zone with a 1,600 and then see what happens on a different day if our hamster does several 1,600 meter repeats?

With the fatigue from his 800s still there, he kept his legs rolling along at a nice steady 88-89 seconds per lap, which if he rests up properly, is close to 5K pace. He reaches his 10K HR goal of 161 a little bit after the 400 meter point.

More importantly, he reaches his 5K HR goal of 166 well before the 800 meter mark (in the first session) and spends *close to 55 percent of his Interval time at 5K HR goal or a little higher.* (Compared to 40 percent during 800s and only 10 percent while running 400s.)

At	Time	HR	*Three*	1st rep	2nd	3rd
200 m		150	*weeks*	154	154	159
400	1.28	160	*later*	162	164	162
600		164	*he*	163	166	164
800	2.57	166	*averaged*	164	169	165
1,200	4.26	168	*5:53 per*	166	169	167
1,600	5.55	168	*1600m*	169	168	166

As you can see from his session a few weeks later, if *you* run mile repeats at 5K pace, you'll probably get over 80 percent of your Interval time at or above 10K heartrate intensity, or 92 % of max HR. 400s at 5K pace only give you about 30 percent of your time at 10K HR or higher).

During the first rep in the second session, he took nearly 1200 meters to reach his 5K heartrate with fresh legs. After a three minute rest, he took less than 600 meters to reach a HR of 166 and spent 64 percent of his rep at or above 166.

Run mile repeats at 5K pace and (last rep aberration aside) you'll spend a huge percentage of training time at your 5K HR goals, and be forced to make improvements to your running efficiency to achieve these sessions.

The lower heartrate in the last column is a reflection of our hamster concentrating on his running efficiency while dealing with his fatigue, and perhaps because he had sweated off some of his over-hydration, so he was at ideal running weight for this final 5:53:42 of running at 5K pace.

You'll spend a greater percentage at your time at 5K HR if you add a fifth lap to get 2,000 meter repeats.

With a sound base and good peaking, many of you could eventually race within 20 seconds per mile of your best 10K. Four time Olympic Champion Emil Zatopek ran a 10,000 meter world record in 28.52; his 20K world record was 59.51. He ran 12 seconds per mile slower for the longer distance. Few readers of this book will be training at Zatopeks' intensity seven days a week. However, many of you will be training at his intensity for three to four sessions a week! Note that Zatopek took 12 years to reach his peak.

British coach Frank Horwill's rule of 4 says you'll slow by 4 seconds per 400 meters when doubling race distance. That's 16 seconds per mile from 10K to a 20K; a fraction more for the half marathon. A bit difficult for slow runners.

The race predictor by Pete Riegel predicts your half marathon to be about 2.223 times your 10K, or 1:14:40 for a 33.35 10K runner. Slowing by 17 seconds per mile from 5:25 per mile to 5:42 for that wonderful sub 75 half. A 1:42:41 for a 46:11 10K runner has you slowing from about 7:27 miles to 7:50s for the half, or by 23 seconds per mile.

Click on "Calculators" at www.runnersworld.com to get a predicted half marathon time based on any race distance.

Always apply the **Aesop Principle** to racing and training, "Steady even pace gives you personal records." Run hills and Intervals at the right pace and start races at the right speed and like the fabled tortoise, you'll be successful.

Many of you will never race farther than the half marathon. Congratulations. As some of you race for longer than Olympic Marathoners, your ideal distance is the half. Enjoy cross-training while racing twice a year each at 5K, 8K, 10K, 10 miles and the half marathon. Enjoy a healthy running lifestyle for decades. Later, if 4 hours is doable, you might want to run a 20-mile race. See page 148.

Chapter Nine

Cross-Training with Weights

Experienced runners get fewer injuries than new runners do, perhaps because they've found out that soft surfaces, regularly replacing running shoes and a steady build-up of training keeps them away from podiatrists and orthopedists.

Despite experience, the strongest predictor of injury risk for runners is weekly mileage. Whether a new or an old hand to this game, if you replace a few of your miles with cross training, you can reduce your long-term injury risk.

As stated in Chapter Six, the 3 pillars of fitness are:

* Cardiovascular training: already covered.
* Flexibility: the stretching in Chapter Six, and
* Strength Training: which we will now explore.

It's easy to rest while bike riding...just enjoy the view as you cruise down a gentle slope, but see pages 139-143.

You rest while running too: Even when you are running fast you're resting! Not all of your muscle cells contract at the same time! Some of your muscle fibers are resting or recovering ready for their next contraction.

Make your individual muscle cells stronger and you'll use even fewer muscle cells to maintain a given speed. Make your muscles stronger and a greater percentage of your muscle fibers will be resting for each microsecond. Get your muscle fibers strong enough and you'll be able to run a 10K at the speed which used to be your 5-mile pace; you may eventually run the 10K at your old 5K pace. You'll also run personal records at the 5K and the half-marathon.

Why should you cross-train?

* To make your running muscles stronger...allowing you to run faster with the same amount of effort.
* To add endurance or muscular efficiency...allowing you to run farther at a given speed.
* To work your non-running muscles. Weight training will keep you fit for your other activities of life.
* To maintain muscle strength as you age. (Inactive people lose about half a pound of muscle per year, or about 10 percent of their muscle mass per decade, decreasing their metabolic rate and increasing likelihood of getting fat.)
* To increase blood volume, which gets more nutrients to your muscles, and takes out lactic acid and carbon dioxide faster, while cooling you more efficiently.
* To decrease injury risk while achieving all of the above.
* To take a break from running for a day or two per week: For emotional (adding variety) or physical reasons.
* To stay fit when injured. You can do monumental workouts while your Achilles or other ailments heal, or just stay fit for life with 50 minutes on five days a week. You can maintain your cardiovascular fitness for years without running a step.

Which type of cross training you choose is dependent upon your goals. Be as specific to running as you can for the best results on your running fitness. Hills and mud running strengthens your muscles. Bounding in sand and double or single leg jumps during which you land on a soft surface with slightly bent knees give you explosive power to improve your running speed.

Pick up your knees for half a dozen striders of 100 to 150 meters twice a week within your easy runs. Don't run faster than mile pace but do practice a relaxed up-tempo pace. After 12 weeks or so of bounding and striders, you'll be ready for less specific strength training.

The best type of cross training to build strong muscle cells is weight training. Strength or resistance training will give your muscle strength a boost and improve endurance for hour plus activities such as half marathon running by 20 percent, and improve your lactate threshold and VO2 max.

During weight training, alternate:

* Pure strength training sessions using fairly heavy weights. Lift slowly for 8 to 10 repeats. Recover while working the antagonist muscle. Example: Pooped out your quadriceps with the leg extension? Walk straight to the Hamstring curl machine and do your 10 repeats there. Then do some chest press or lat. pull downs to rest your legs before doing a set on the leg press machine or half squats.
* Endurance lifting by using more modest weights. Lift a bit faster but with good form for 12 to 16 repeats. Cruise yet don't rush between machines to keep your heartrate up.

To make sure that you stress all of your muscle fibers, you can hold the weights at maximum resistance for several seconds. For example, the leg extension. After 6 repeats using a flowing action while lifting and lowering the weight every 5 to 7 seconds, on the 7th effort, hold the weight up with extended legs for a count of five seconds. Feel your quadriceps muscles tension prior to relaxing the weight down. Do two more of this hold the weight static type exercise before finishing with 3 to 4 of the rhythmic efforts. Over ensuing sessions, aim for half of your efforts to be the lift and hold type. You'll force all of your muscle fibers to work because the keenest fibers, which usually do the initial work, are forced to rest.

Slow-motion option

A variation on the lift and hold technique is to completely exhaust your muscle fibers with the so-called "slow-lift or slow-motion style." Do each lift over about 14 seconds: it requires substantial effort during the work phase as you lift up or pull down over 7 seconds instead of 3 or 4 seconds. It takes work and control during the relaxation phase as you let the weight return to its start point over 7 seconds. Once you've done several sessions, the last rep is supposed to be a nail biting slog as you work over maybe 30 seconds to do one last repeat. You stay at each exercise for 3 to 4 minutes in order to exhaust that muscle group.

Slow-lift is not for the new weight trainer. This is maximum weight training, can lead to severe muscle aches, and if you follow its proponents suggestions, it takes almost a week to recover from. Their goal is to create such a high level of fatigue that you only do this session once a week.

It's rather like running 20 miles in one run when your longest run each week used to be 5 miles, and your total mileage is 25 per week. It takes you at least a week to recover from that 20 mile run! If you don't get injured, you'll merely suffer all week with achy muscles and you will not be able to run for that week, plus you will have defeated Yakovlev's principle.

Completely exhaust a muscle with slow-move and you will not want to repeat the session for a week.

Slow lift proponents say you can get a whole body session with 6 exercises. My gym has six exercise machines for the arm and shoulder muscles, so getting the entire body fit with one session of 6 lifts is a wacky idea. My gym also has 6 machines for the leg muscles and three for the trunk. I use all 15 machines, plus a few exercises in the free weights room! One set takes me about 30 minutes. Of course, 30 minutes per week is more than most people exercise for anyway, so slow-lift will get some takers. So will the three minutes per day home gyms sold by infomercials!

The six exercises recommended are:

* Leg extension and leg curl;
* Hip adduction and hip abduction;

* Low back extension and abdominal curl;
* Chest press, shoulder press and compound row;
* Lateral raise and latissimi pull down;
* Biceps curl and triceps extension;

This list, of course, is actually 13 exercises, and you'll need to add the leg press, plus calf raises and abdominal crunches to exercise closer to your whole body. Whether you go for 7 seconds work and 7 seconds relaxing the weight down, or 10 seconds of slow work and 4 seconds relaxing the weight down, it will take you 3 minutes per exercise.

A recent article said this session should take no more than 25 minutes. At 3 minutes each, the basic 13 exercises will take you 39 minutes, plus the time between exercises to move to and set the right weight; it's 48 minutes for the complete 16 exercises, plus set up time.

With slow movement, you'll need to lift 75 to 80 percent of your usual weight the first few times you do 12 reps.

Slow lift works for three main reasons:

* Your muscle fibers repeatedly fire during your 7 to 10 second lift. They learn to contract on short rests.
* Your reluctant muscle fibers, which let others do the work, are forced to contract once the early fibers fatigue.
* Little assistance from momentum. Starting up movement, or the first inch of lifting a weight is the hardest. Every inch of movement is tough with slow-lift.

The lift and hold for five seconds (page 110) gives a more modest muscle burn, and you can add one rep per week until it is too much to recover from in two or three days, or it interferes with your run the next day. After a month, add another pair of repeats or a little more weight.

Alternatively, try this <u>drop down</u> variation to fatigue your muscle fibers.

Lets say that you lift 50 pounds using the biceps curl for 12 repeats and it gets you nicely tired. Like a sensible runner, you could have lifted two more times. Instead, drop the weight down to 40 pounds and do six reps. It will take a couple seconds to adjust, but try six more reps with 30 pounds. If you give muscle fibers minimal recovery before lifting the reduced weights, your fairly fatigued muscles will have to use all of their reserve fibers to achieve the lift. Maintain good form and your injury risk is low.

Use this weight reduction series for one shoulder and one leg exercise the first session. Two days later, try a different upper and different lower body exercise. For the third session go back to your normal routine.

Spice up your second week by trying both upper body and both leg exercises for one session, and do another machine for each area of the body in the second session. Add two machines per week until you're doing the "weight reduction series" for all machines, for one session per week.

Normally take 25 minutes to do 15 different machines? Expect to take 40 minutes for this more stimulating session.

After 12 weeks using any style of lifting weights, you may find that you're ready to increase the amount you lift. Don't add much. Five pounds is usually enough, and reduce the number of repeats for your first new session.

Whatever style of lifting ends up dominating, count upwards. Counting up the number of reps you've done is a positive approach to exercise. You expect to do 12 repeats, so get the sense of achievement as you reach your goal. Counting down from 12 to zero is a negative system. Only four to go; only three to go. It's better to achieve 8 lifts; achieve 9 lifts. Use the same positive approach for speed running by counting the number of repeats toward achieving your set of eight 400s instead of counting down.

Weight Training for Body Balance and to decrease injuries or recover from injury, to lose weight and to run faster!

Weight training increases your muscle mass, which increases the number of calories you burn per day. One extra pound of muscle will burn 40 to 50 calories every day. That will be worth 5 pounds of weight loss each year simply by owning an extra pound of muscle. You need strong muscles to run fast. Weight training also increases tendon and ligament strength and bone density, thus reducing injury risk.

Weight training decreases your risk of osteoporosis and most other diseases described in Appendix IV. You'll build more lean tissue, i.e. muscle, which means a higher metabolic rate, which leads to more calories burned every day. Your body fat percentage will of course decrease.

Weight training also improves your glucose metabolism, your sense of balance, digestion, mood and sleep pattern.

Weight training does not take much time. One set with each lift will build more than 75 percent of the muscle which three sets would!

Should you use weight machines or free weights? Use both of course.

Exercising at home? Free weights are the obvious choice, or you can invest in one machine with a gazillion exercises...which will hide under your bed!

Belong to a gym? Weight training machines reduce injury risk because they force you to be positioned fairly safely, making you lift with good form. With machines, you can target individual muscles. No weights to fall off the bar either. Machines also limit your sideways movement.

Free weights do offer flexibility, giving you a total body workout. Your supporting muscles have to make minor adjustments to keep you balanced...they'll have to work too.

You do squats primarily to work the leg muscles. Hold dumbbells or a barbell and you'll be working your arms a bit, plus your back and abdominals to maintain your balance. You can work the smallish muscles more readily with free weights. Bicep curls are fine for the ugh biceps, but by turning the hands inward you can give more work to the brachialis muscles.

You do not need three hour long sessions humping huge weights to get stronger. Watch a typical 3-hour weight training guy, and he or she spends most of the time resting between near maximum lifts. Thirty minutes of gentle weight training two times per week will give runners most of the gains available from weight training.

Do 12 reps of an exercise for the front muscle such as the biceps, take a leisurely 10 seconds to adjust the next machine, and do 12 reps for the posterior muscle or triceps. Then move efficiently to a leg or abdominal machine before returning your rested arm muscles to say a latissimi pull-down or chest press.

The supermarket is the best place to find your first dumbbells. Partial to bottled water? Fill two 16-ounce bottles to the very top with tap water to get slightly over one pound for each hand.

Orange juice your tonic? Get a pair of 32-ounce and 48-ounce containers, and you'll get 2 and 3 pound weights.

Feeling strong after a month or so of weight training? Add sand to another pair of wide neck water and juice containers to easily reach 10 pounds and more. Check the actual weight and mark the containers. Still weight training after 12 weeks? Buy some vinyl-coated dumbbells in one pound increments.

While a weight bench is useful for doing the bench press, press-ups work fine for most people.

The Actual Weight Training:

Do your weight training wisely...do many reps, using modest amounts of weight--about 60 percent of the maximum which you can lift. The American College of Sports Medicine recommends:

At least eight separate exercises for different muscle groups. Do two or more sets of 8 to 12 repeats for each exercise and lift at least twice a week.

Use free weights to bring your balancing muscles into play, but use good lifting technique.

Breathe in a normal way. Don't hold your breath.

Note: Most people breathe out during the work phase, and in during the recovery phase. Don't think about it; do what's natural for you.

Do **triceps and biceps curls** for the arm muscles. The biceps is at the front of the upper arm. While stood up with good posture, hold a dumbbell with your arm at your side. Keeping the elbow and shoulder still, bring the dumbbell up toward your shoulder, and then ease it back down to your side. The movement is around your elbow joint, not a rhythmic waist or chest and shoulder movement because you're trying to lift too much weight! Isolate those biceps to develop them. Use a weight you can lift 10 to 12 times, then exercise the other arm. Doing both arms at the same time is more time efficient, but stay focused. Placing your shoulders against a wall decreases shoulder roll.

You can do the bicep curl with a barbell but it has potential for stressing the back. Using dumbbells while sitting on the incline bench is probably the safest technique. Your back gets support and the sitting angle encourages you to move the weight without rolling your shoulders.

For the triceps, the muscle behind your arm, you'll need to start with your belly in a horizontal position. Lying on a bench works, provided your shoulder is just over the edge. Or do bent over kickbacks, in which you support yourself with your non-working arm while leaning over to get your belly horizontal to the earth's surface. Bring the dumbbell to your shoulder, raise the elbow to get the upper arm parallel to the ground, then keeping the shoulder and elbow still, straighten your lower arm through its range of motion taking the dumbbell past your butt. Then swing the dumbbell sedately back round to your shoulder.

Do the same number of reps with each arm, then do another set of biceps curls and repeat the triceps too. Build to three sets if you like. As with most weight lifting, you can hold the position of maximum strain for a few seconds, or keep the movement really slow: it's up to you.

Triceps extensions also isolate the back of the arms, but there is the potential for hitting your head with the dumbbell. So, use one dumbbell in the sitting or standing position. Hold it with both hands above your head. Hug the back of your ears with your upper arm, and lower the weight behind you. Gradually straighten your arms and repeat. Do your usual 10 to 12 repeats. You can also do arm dips holding onto a sturdy chair for the triceps. Use the triceps press-down machine too.

The **deltoids** cover your shoulder joint and give you a nicely padded look if developed properly. Raising the arms up from the side of your body until they are horizontal, while holding light dumbbells work the medial deltoids.

Raise your arms up to your front and you'll be working the front or anterior part of the deltoids. You achieve better results if prone on an incline bench at 60 degrees. Start with your arms dangling while holding dumbbells and lift them up and out to shoulder height. Don't lock out at the elbow. Push your arms behind and up to work the posterior deltoid.

The vertical arm press is done in the sitting position with shoulders directly above your hips and back straight. Start with a barbell at chin height with your elbows flexed and push it above your head to work the middle and anterior deltoid, plus the trapezius.

The bench-press is unlikely to go out of fashion for developing pec power. Figure out what you can easily manage to lift because the weight is going to be just above your noggin. Lie with your back flat against the bench. Push the barbell up and you've got the same motion as a military press-up. Keep one or two reps in reserve, then there's little danger of dropping the weight on yourself.

Avoid the barbell trapping you during the bench press by using a dumbbell in each hand. You'll work both sides evenly and you can drop them in emergencies. Better yet, lift 80 percent of your maximum reps: Keep a bit in reserve.

The pull-up or chin-up is for stronger types. After a complete warm up, use a bench to get yourself into the up position. Hold the bar with your palms facing you, and then keep your body straight as you lower yourself down. Don't rock and roll. Simply lift yourself back up to touch the bar and lower your body again.

Do the latissimi pull-down, plus the push-up for the rest of the shoulders and upper back.

You can do all of these arm and shoulder exercises with machines. However, weight-bearing exercises give greater rewards because you have to make constant muscle adjustments when using free weights.

The Press-Up or Push-Up is the simplest way to train your upper body muscles, giving pecs, deltoids, triceps and biceps a good workout. As with running, form is important.

* Don't let your stomach and hips sag down;
* Don't strain with your head back or down;
* Do tighten your abdominal muscles; and
* Do keep your body in a straight line as you push your body up with your arms and as you lower yourself.
* Stop when form is difficult to maintain. Don't do one extra press-up, because that's the one which injures you.

Your first press-up.

Do some gentle warm up exercises and stretching, lie on your belly with your hands under your shoulders, fingers pointing either forward or inward, which means your elbows are bent. Legs should be straight behind you with your feet a few inches apart to give a four-point base.

Lift those knees off the floor a bit and tuck your toes up toward your hips. You'll be supporting yourself on the balls of your feet. Training shoes or barefoot, it's up to you. Squeeze those abdominals as you prepare to lift yourself up in a straight line by tightening your chest muscles and biceps to straighten your arms. Don't lock out the elbows at the top; keep some movement in reserve. Don't allow the shoulders to move in toward the head.

Ease your body back down until your upper arms are parallel to the floor. Touch the surface with your nose instead of your chin to keep your neck relaxed, then slowly raise yourself up again. Build up to 3 sets of 10 to 15.

Shoulders not strong enough for the full press-up? Rest the knees on the surface and do the push-ups in a straight line...which means lifting less weight. Or, use the seat of a study chair, or bench for your hands, but support yourself on the balls of your feet as in the full press-up. Arms at table height works too; practice good form for a few weeks, and then proceed to chair height and perhaps the floor.

The mid-section.

Do sit-ups or crunches to help your posture. Stomach muscles are weaker than back muscles. Always tighten the abdominal muscles before the movement, and avoid the Ab machines which make sit-ups easier because the exercise is then less effective. Include some twisting trunk curls to work the oblique muscles. As you lift your shoulders forward, twist to take your left elbow toward your right knee; on the next rep do right elbow to left knee.

True crunches restrict the movement to the first few inches to isolate the upper abs. Lie on a comfortable surface. Place your feet flat on the mat. With your hands touching your ears, lift your head, shoulders and upper back a few inches off of the surface with tightened abs.

A nice sit-up variation is to bring one knee up above your hip, then raise your shoulders toward that knee. Do both knees of course and keep the movement nice and slow to work on the way up and on the way back down.

Swimming, with the dolphin kick also works your abs, as does standing or sitting up straight! Tighten those muscles for 3 to 5 seconds for half a dozen reps several times a day.

The seated leg tuck gives the lower abdominals and the hip flexors gentle exercise. Sit back on a bench or recliner chair and close your eyes. Still awake? Raise your feet a couple inches off of the floor. Bend your knees, bring them up toward your chest, and push your upper torso forward.

Use a ball for exercise? Place the ball against a wall and your back against the ball. Extend your legs out with heels resting on the floor. Contract your abs and tilt your pelvis up to raise your hips and bring your body into a straight line. Hold for a few seconds then ease down without arching your back to the starting position.

Alternatively, lean your back into the ball with your butt close to the edge, knees a bit higher than your butt and your feet flat on the floor. With shins and thighs at right angles, tighten your abs and extend your arms over your head while you almost straighten your legs. Pull yourself back over to work the abs. You can also do curls or sit-ups on the ball.

Try these trunk exercises from John Brennand, the multiple United States National Masters Gold Medalist on road, cross-country and track, and the 2,002 65-69 age group 10,000 meter track Champion.

Start by kneeling on the ground, resting your weight on forearms and knees. Raise your left arm and right leg to a horizontal position; hold them parallel to the floor for a count of five, and return to the starting position. Do two sets of 10 for each pair of appendages.

The kneeling back-kick does wonders for the lower back and hip muscles. Kneel on a bench, with your back straight and hands holding the side of the bench. Allow one leg to hang down loosely but straight, then raise that leg as far up behind you as you can. Do 10 to 15 reps with each leg, and several sets can be your goal.

You can also do a version of the banana or spinal extension from page 81. Lie on the floor with arms stretched out beyond your head. Lift the right arm and left leg for 5 seconds, then ease down and do the left arm and right leg. You can also lift all 4 limbs at the same time or do it when lying on a ball.

And of course, the Leg Muscles.

According to top runner John Brennand, "Strengthening exercises are particularly important for masters runners.

"Stride frequency is the same, but stride length decreases with age after the mid forties. We run slower because we are not as strong. We run more efficiently if the body is stronger." Brennand recommends this upper leg exercise.

Single Leg Drop.

Stand on one leg, on a bench or low chair about knee height. While standing upright, bend your supporting leg until you touch the ground with the toe of your resting leg. Without an assist from the restive leg, push your body back up. Keep the body as upright as possible. Do 3 sets of 10. After a few weeks, you can hold weights to add resistance.

Half Squats work the same area as the leg-press machine. For both exercises, keep your knees in line with your toes, and don't let the knees go farther forward than the toes: in essence, you sit back with tight abs, a straight back, but the shins stay almost perpendicular to the ground.

With feet shoulder width apart for balance, use hand weights early, a lightly weighted barbell across your upper back when you've become skilled. Dropped dumbbells are less likely to damage you if you lose your balance. A half-inch heel boost may help you to maintain balance. Bend at the knees while keeping the back erect. Go down slowly to your knees level of comfort; thighs will typically be parallel to the floor. Your muscles work on the way down and on the way up! Safer half squats can be done standing in front of a bench or chair. Lightly touch the bench at the lowest point of each rep and then push up quite fast.

Traditional Leg Lunges. Start with feet together. Take a step forward, drop down into the lunge as if you're in a sword fight. Keep your back straight by contracting your abdominals while lifting your chest. Balance your body weight between your feet; the front foot should be flat on the ground and you'll be on the ball of the rear foot.

While pushing back up to the standing position, simultaneously squeeze your buttocks and thigh muscles to pull yourself back up. (Description continued on page 123.)

Alternate legs or do a dozen with the left followed by a dozen with the right as the lead leg. You can also do the reverse lunge by stepping back to stretch the hip flexors, while working the hamstrings, quadriceps and buttocks.

The lunge is a test of your balance. Take short steps forward early on, and hold on lightly to the back of a chair if necessary. As your balance improves, dispense with the chair, take a longer lunge, then hold light hand weights and move up to dumbbells to increase the resistance on the legs.

The Smith Machine Stationary Lunge requires less skill at balancing, because you keep the torso in the same line. Rest the barbell across your shoulders. Take half a stride back with the left leg and half a stride forward with the right. As you drop down, the thigh of the left leg points toward the floor, the lower leg is parallel to the floor and you'll be on the ball of that foot. The front leg's thigh is parallel to the floor, and the lower leg is perpendicular to the floor, with the foot flat.

Set the Smith Bar at an appropriate height and you can do partial weight bearing pull-ups and triceps dips. Place a bench under your butt for your start point.

The **side lunge** is a great way to bring the gracilis muscle and other adductors and the abductors into play (the hammies and quads work too). Start by holding light dumbbells at your side. With your right foot facing front, step to the side with your left leg. Point the left toes at 45 degrees, and bend the knee until it's over the left ankle. Keep the torso erect, but feel a nice stretch in your inner thigh as you lower yourself down. Do 10 to 20 reps, and switch legs.

Old faithful Step-ups. Using a bench, chair or a pair of steps about 18 inches high, step up with one leg. Straighten this lead leg to pull yourself up. Step down slowly with the lead leg. Unless specifically working them, don't push off with the calf muscles. Change lead leg after 20 reps. If that's too tame for you, hold a small dumbbell in each hand.

Want to work the lower back along with your hammies and gluts? Try the **Bent-legged dead lift.**

Standing with your feet shoulder width apart, bend at the knees and lower your arms with a hip rotation while keeping your back straight. Pick up your barbell or dumbbells and bring them to shin height. As with squats, keep your eyes focused on something at head height. Keep that back straight as you push up with your legs and rotate through the hips to stand up straight. The weights end up at thigh height. Bend your knees, lower your shoulders with a straight back to your start position, and do 8 to 12 reps.

The above exercises work the quadriceps, hamstrings and gluteals: the power muscles for running.

Machines allow you to isolate a particular muscle group. Leg extensions, hamstring curls and the leg press cover your upper leg muscles. Use the abductor and adductor machine to stay balanced. Do the calf muscle machine with knees almost locked, then a set with the knees bent at 45 degrees to work both of the calf muscles.

You don't need a gym to exercise your hammies. Sit on an office chair with wheels. Sit up straight now! Adjust the seat height to get your feet flat on the floor...then drop the seat another inch. Lift your lower legs and place your heals 6 to 12 inches in front of you. Pull yourself forward, then "walk" your chair around the room while staying seated. Feel those hamstrings work. Do single leg walks too.

Here's Brennand's favorite lower leg exercise

Stand on a low step or staircase with the right foot on the higher level, and your weight on the left forefoot at the lower level. Using the right foot for balance, bounce rapidly ten times on the left foot. Do three sets of ten for each foot.

Or do...**Heel Raises**.

Stand on the balls of your feet on a two inch block or a stair. Raise your heels up by contracting your calves, then roll up onto your toes. Drop slowly back down so that the heel dips below the step. Keep a steady and rhythmic movement. Do single leg raises for still stronger calves. Do calf stretches too! Note: Too much of this exercise can strain the plantar fascia or the Achilles tendon.

The above two exercises work the gastrocnemius and soleus, which extends the foot and give power at stride-off.

Alphabet or numbers and Shin Lift.

While sitting in a chair, raise your feet and write the alphabet or zero to nine several times with your toes.

In a similar position, or sitting on a table, use a weight around your foot. Move the foot up and down at the ankle. This is often called the paint-pot exercise. Or place a dumbbell on your toes and lift it up using your shin muscles.

While Lydiard felt that hill training was the only beneficial resistance training for runners, you can develop calf endurance by skipping rope. Although you'll work the upper leg muscles and arms, the calf muscles do most of the work. Oddly enough, it's mainly the calf muscles which propel you forward in running! Wear sturdy shoes on a forgiving surface. Build up slowly over several weeks and stop if you feel leg pains. Ten minutes of skipping burns about 100 calories; do three sessions per week and that's 5 pounds of fat every year.

"It takes months of regular weights and resistance training before you see results," says Brennand, "Do make it a regular part of your training."

Remember to include shoulder exercises. One of the simplest shoulder training exercises is to hold a light dumbbell in each hand and swing the arms at high speed as if sprinting up hill. Push your hands behind you and encourage the momentum to carry your arms forward. The emphasis is to push back rather than punch the air to your front. This exercise makes up for the lack of shoulder work during elliptical training and bike rides in Chapter Ten.

<u>Protein Debate:</u> Building muscle requires protein but not supplements. Most people in western society get more than 150 percent of the recommended daily allowance (RDA) for protein. Eat a balanced diet with a quality protein source 4 to 5 times per day and you'll have plenty of the building bricks (amino acids) to form large muscles. You'll gain less than an ounce (28 grams) per day of muscle with weight training, so 75 to 105 grams of protein daily will give you plenty of bricks. A high protein diet is dehydrating and it's cruel to your kidneys.

Fruit and vegetables keep you healthy with vitamins, minerals and antioxidants. Citrus fruits, berries, kiwi and the melon clan, green and yellow veggies, beans and grains give a foundation to your carbohydrate and vitamin intake.

Drinking non-fat milk, yogurt smoothies or eating low fat energy bars straight after exercise helps your muscles to recover from all types of training. Your muscles need a hit of carbohydrate and a little protein to begin their recovery.

Use any style of non-fat milk, including chocolate, or yogurt, or non-fat soy milk for your smoothie's protein source. Add a fruit juice, three servings of whole fruit and some ice chips, then blend, and you've got 75 grams or so of carbohydrate, plus 10 to 15 grams of protein to start your muscles re-fueling. Texture the smoothie to your taste.

Gentle aerobic exercise after weight training sessions also flushes your muscles with nutrient rich blood, which sets you up for the next workout in which you give a moderate stress to a different aspect of your fitness.

Don't overtrain with weight lifting. Don't jump into three sets of lifting 80 pounds when your maximum single lift is 90 pounds. Don't insult your body with unrealistic amounts of weight training. Note: Most runners should be aiming for 15 repeats of each exercise because you need endurance and strength. Leg muscles respond well to 20 reps per set.

Chapter Ten

Aerobic or Cardiovascular Cross Training.

Add a couple of bicycle rides or elliptical sessions to Chapter Nine's strength training...and oxen will be jealous of your power. Develop the strength which helps you to maintain running form (or biomechanics) and running speed despite your race fatigue.

As stated early in Chapter Nine, cross training decreases injury risk while maintaining or increasing endurance. Whichever type of aerobic cross training exercise you do, build up slowly. After many weeks, incorporate a series one to five minute efforts at modest intensity to stimulate your cardiovascular system. If you find you really like cross-training, aim for 3 to 5 minute intervals at 5K intensity and 10 to 15 minute repeats at 15K effort. Otherwise:

* You can do 15 minutes cross training as a warm-up before running;
* On hot or cold days do 40 minutes as a substitute for running;
* Do it as your cooldown with a drink by your side.

Be specific. It takes quality running to run well. The rule of "specificity of training" states that:

To run a good half-marathon, you must run significant mileage within one and a half minutes per mile of your half marathon pace, and some miles at faster than race pace. Most of your cross training must mimic running as much as possible to be effective.

Your aerobic capacity will increase if you add any old cross training...without decreasing your run workouts. However, if your cross training is specific enough, you can also get the same training benefit when using it as a substitute for running.

Cross training exercise goals include:

* Weight bearing: Avoid sitting if possible. Rowing machines are poor. If you stand for uphill biking...fine. Elliptical trainers are even better.
* Beat the weather: Biking and pool work are excellent on hot days. Set up fans indoors and regulate the temperature to use most types of machine. Running on a treadmill is not cross training but it keeps you off the ice. Set up your bicycle on bike rollers and you'll have cross training away from the ice.
* Variety: See some different scenery and cover greater distances with higher wind flow to cool you while biking, or have company while using exercise machines at the gym.
* Recovery from runs: Yesterdays session should have been light enough that you can cruise 15 miles for pleasure today, but you can still substitute 60 minutes of cross training instead. Remember to mimic running, ensure that it's relaxing, yet get your heartrate up. You should plan on complete rest days from exercise too.
* Reduce the impact on your joints. Land softly and avoid overstriding to reduce the affects of ground impact on every stride. However, run in the pool too.
* Increase your training: Give your muscles extra training while still running your 40 or 60 miles per week.

* Stay fit when injured: Some cross-training exercise options should be available if you have a running injury.

Because running is endurance focused, after weight training, the 2nd through 4th choice for cross training goes to activities of a continuous nature. All three options give huge rewards for:

* Recovery from runs.
* Add-ons to the end of a run, or the warm-up prior to running.
* Substitute for a run.
* Non or low-impact quality training.
* And of course, for additional training.

Choose the activities which you like because you're more likely to do them. Fitness training requires consistent training. You need three or four main quality sessions of running or cross training, plus several other sessions to make you fit enough to train long or hard on those three main training days.
The three best aerobic exercises for runners:

Choice One: Deep Water Running.

Doesn't sound like cross-training, but because you've eliminated the ground impact, water running is clearly the best alternative to land running. For most of us, it means running in a pool. Keep it interesting by having a companion, listening to music, or by doing gentle intervals at threshold or 5K intensity. Pool running is substantially more running muscle specific than swimming.

Pool running works most of your muscles. Unlike elliptical training and biking, it gives a significant workout for the arms: You work your arms exactly the same way as you do for land running! Your arms also have to work against the water's resistance, so pool running gives a great cardiorespiratory workout.

You can pool run while recuperating from most running injuries such as Tendonitis, stress fractures, ankle and knee problems. Fail to address the cause, and injuries may return a few weeks after you switch back to land running. You may:

* Need different shoes;
* Need to run on softer surfaces;
* Need to correct your running form;
* Need cross-training for 20 to 40 percent of your training;
* Need to give your body time to catch up with or adapt to your training.

Acute muscle injuries will usually need total rest for a few days, but many people can then commence gentle pool running. It's easy to strain your muscles during pool running, so practice restraint when pool running with recently strained muscles.

Because of the hydrostatic pressure which forces blood back into your heart, your heart pushes out more blood per stroke when you're in water. Your heartrate is therefore lower when exercising in the wet stuff. To get the equivalent training effect as land running, your intensity needs to feel a bit harder. Your heartrate will still be lower. You still don't need to run at mile pace intensity. Gentle intervals mean doing 2-mile effort in water to get 5K training intensity; run 10K effort to get 15K intensity.

Pick intervals of one to 10 minutes and do them at harsher than land running effort. Run at speed for the same total length of time which you would normally do. Drink fluids every 10 to 15 minutes if the session (including your weights and other cross training) lasts over an hour.

You can work on your flexibility with pool running. Pool running does tend to over emphasize the hip flexors and extensors, while resting the weight bearing calves and quadriceps muscles. This also means you are not building up the calves and quads! Be sure to match every 40-minute pool session with a few minutes of weight training for the calves and quadriceps muscles.

Maintain good running form by leaning forward only slightly or remaining upright with your head up. Swing those arms just as much as you would during land running. Your hands should be lightly clenched and come up no higher than nipple height, which means they stay under water. It is probably even better if you don't see your hands come up in front of you. Keep them closer to waist height for faster cadence. Push them back to slightly behind your butt and keep the motion forward and backward.

Do most pool running in deep water so that your feet don't touch the bottom. A flotation vest helps to take the strain off your shoulders and allows you to work on running form. If you also do exercises in the shallow end such as jumping exercises for your calf muscles, use aquatic shoes or those old sturdy sandals which you used to walk up Mount Whitney! You can work the calf muscles at their most important skill...pushing you forward on each stride. Do a few minutes of easy pool running to finish off.

Need a break after half of your intervals? Lie on your back and kick with your legs as if swimming backstroke. Then give the hamstrings a bonus workout by pulling yourself back up the pool on your back while flipping your ankles rapidly to your buttocks.

Water is a great non-impact training opportunity.

Pool running saves your muscles, tendons and joints for a longer running life. You can take your hip flexors and extensors through a huge range of motion, but you will not damage yourself from the over-striding impact. Use water running wisely. Don't jump into a session the day before your main speed training session. You can easily fatigue your hip flexors during your first pool run, so save the pool for the day after speed training.

Think about your running motion. You'll soon develop bad running form if you do high training volume in water. Use a running vest if it feels right for you, though some people think the vest restricts their movement. Vestless running generally forces you to exercise harder. If you're after a low intensity exercise session, wearing a vest is a wise choice. Training hard in the pool? Give the vest a miss after you've warmed up.

Don't restrict pool running to rest days. You can run one of your hard sessions at threshold pace or VO2 maximum effort in the pool each week: The next day do your easy and pleasure seeking running on land.

Water running is also an opportunity to add a half session of training or to take an easy day. Feeling really tired this week? Instead of your fairly typical 4 times one mile at 10K pace or 16 times 400 meters at 5K pace, head to the pool. Do 2 x 8 minutes quite hard, or 6 x two minutes slightly harder. For the average half-marathon runner, this would be half of the normal track session. Add the fact that it's non-impact, and you should feel refreshed the next time you run.

The pool session could also be done as an extra session the day after speedwork. Add a short, modest quality pool session to your 2 weekly land speed sessions to give yourself two and a half speed sessions a week. Do this only on alternate weeks, and there's minimal over training potential.

Chapter 9 said that you get 75 % of the strength benefits from one set of weight training that you get from three sets. When doing Intervals you also get 75 % of the running benefits from the first half of a pool running session!

Live close to a sandy beach or wash? A pleasant variation to reduce ground impact is to run though 6 to 12 inches of water at a variety of paces, with or without an old pair of running shoes. Benefits include:

* You have to lift your knees to avoid falling so you'll get a bounding type exercise for strength.
* The water cushions your landing.
* The sand or shale cushions your landing still more.
* The ground moves away from you at push-off.
* The splashed water is cooling, so: You could alternate a 3 minute fast effort on the firm sandbar, with 3 minutes easy pace running through shallow water, followed by a minute of fast water running, then repeat.
* Hopefully, there will be a few deep spots which you can fall into. Training should be fun.
* You have to work to lift those wet shoes.

Swimming.

You're in the pool, so I owe it to you to discuss swimming as cross-training. If water running is available, don't swim. If you really enjoy swimming though, go ahead.

Running uses mostly leg muscles for power and propulsion. Surprised you with that one, didn't I? Swimming uses about 80 percent upper body muscles to move you through the water.

* Used as a rest, swimming can keep you away from training.
* Used to build your shoulder and arm muscles, swimming can be used as training!

Though they are not mutually exclusive, you probably need to decide whether rest or training is your goal. Apart from diving starts, your fastest five meters of swimming is after you push off from the wall...for every length of the pool. Want to rest your legs for running? Push off gently at each turn and pick up speed using your arms and shoulders.

Want to work your gluteals, hamstrings, quadriceps and calf muscles? Push off strongly and rapidly and you've got a leg press against the waters resistance as you reverse momentum and reach maximum speed in mere hundredths of a second. Extend the push off through your toes like you would at full stride for the calf muscles. You can also give more emphasis to your legs by holding a float with your hands for extensive sessions of kicking. Why do that when you can run in the pool?

Going to swim? Alternate freestyle or frontcrawl with backstroke to balance your session. Breaststroke puts too much strain upon the knees and butterfly is too technical, plus it requires and stimulates excessive shoulder power.

Stimulate the cardiorespiratory system by breathing every 3 to 5 strokes instead of the every 2 strokes which fast swimming would need.

Swim at easy effort. Just like with running, don't get severely out of breath in the early sessions. Be gentle with yourself until you develop a feel for the water, then try:

Interval Training with 50 to 100 meters of fast swimming, alternating with slow swimming, or with 30 seconds rest. Do up to 8 repeats.

I like to do 6 lengths at a time. Two of frontcrawl, one of backcrawl and repeat. I breathe every 4 strokes during the first couple of sets, and every 6 strokes toward the end of the session. After the 30 second rest from the second set, I also do a 12-stroke cycle for the first pool length of each set. This swim session usually comes after weights and elliptical training.

As with pool running, your heartrate will be lower during swimming compared to land running.

Unless you're planning a triathlon, speed is not your main goal, aquadynamics and swimming trunks are out; baggy shorts will do. Do learn how to swim efficiently though to decrease shoulder injury risk. Lead with the top of your head while looking down at the bottom of the pool. Lean on your chest so that your lower body floats high in the water. Don't plash. Extend your arm well forward, and slip it into the water without making waves.

Choice Two: Elliptical Trainer.

Elliptical workouts are the second best aerobic cross training option for runners, easily ahead of biking because you stand for all of your training. Provided you don't place excessive weight on your hands, and exercise at the same intensity, elliptical training will give you the same heartrate and oxygen consumption as treadmill running.

Elliptical training is a cross between cycling, running and stair-climbing, but:

* No traffic or road rage worries and almost zero impact;
* While standing up. Which means your muscles work and weight bear at the same time;
* Elliptical machines are more rhythmic than stair climbers;
* You can work the antagonistic muscles by exercising backwards. Continue to face the front of the machine, but move the legs in reverse mode as if running backwards.

Scientifically, the ground impact forces for elliptical training are equal to the ground impact of walking, or about one tenth the impact of running. Keep your motion rhythmic on a well-balanced machine and your wear and tear is essentially zero...provided you vary the settings on your machine. Just like in biking, you're placing strain upon your joints with every cycle of the legs: vary the amount of flexion at the ankle and knees, by spending two or three minutes at several crossramp levels. After warming up, you can give the calves and Achilles a thorough stretching by using a high incline for several minutes.

The movement on these machines is a gentle ellipse, giving a smooth, rolling action without actual impact. It is great for avoiding injuries, or to maintain fitness while your joints and muscles heal. You can also do most of these suggested elliptical sessions on a stair-climber, but watch out for knee trouble on the stairs.

Note: Resistance and workload or workrate, and effort level are interchangeable phrases for elliptical machines.

The same holds true for crossramp angle, incline, steepness or elevation level.

Buying an elliptical trainer?

Test drive them. Different models have different egg shapes to their ellipse. Some machines allow arm movement with hand levers, giving you upper body exercise: If your arms are moving, you can maintain high heartrates with more modest effort from your leg muscles, which is ideal for rest days. The levers can also be locked in place if the training emphasis is to be the legs.

Runners with good balance can swing their arms instead of holding on to the supports that most machines possess. Got poor balance? Exercise at an intensity which allows you to stay on your feet with only a light low-stress grip on the side rails or handles. Stand up straight with that beautiful belly of yours pulled in. Ease into sessions with all parts of your body relaxed. Hold your head and shoulders up and no slouching.

Elliptical Training Sessions:

Done your 30 minutes of weight training? After all, it's the most important cross training! Then you're ready for the elliptical trainer. To avoid sudden changes in training, spend about 4 weeks getting used to the machine for 10 and building to 30 minutes at a time, using slight variations in resistance and incline to ease the tension on your knees and to get a fuller range of motion. Then after a gentle transition from weights to elliptical for five minutes, try these:

Session One: Do 2 minutes going forward at a comfortable elevation and resistance while maintaining 90 strides (90 for each foot that is) per minute.

Then do 2 minutes with a backwards motion while facing the front of the machine. Use the same elevation, but because the hamstrings are supposed to be weaker than the thigh muscles, your workrate may need to be one or two notches lower.

Continue to alternate 2 minutes forward and backward, but increase the elevation one notch every 2 minutes until it becomes difficult to maintain with a relaxed motion. Then take it back one notch.

At 10 and 15 minutes, you might also increase the resistance a notch. Aim for your exercise intensity to reach anaerobic threshold (15K running effort) at 20 minutes, then maintain it for 5 more minutes.

For your warmdown, ease back on the elevation by one notch each minute while continuing to alternate the forward and backward motion every two minutes. Decrease the resistance also for the last two minutes.

Hint: When changing direction, ease to a stop over several seconds, adjust the resistance, and then recommence as if changing gently from a walk to easy running over several seconds. It's rather like going into reverse on your car. You need to go through neutral before applying the gas.

Session Two: First 10 minutes as for session one, then:

Increase tempo to 100 strides per minute for one minute, ease back to 90 strides to cruise for one minute, change direction and repeat. Then, increase resistance or elevation by one notch for one minute at 100 strides. Rest at the original resistance, change direction and repeat.

Then use 2 followed by 3 additional notches of resistance or elevation to give yourself 8 intervals...4 in each direction.

Do a four-minute warmdown similar to session one.

Your goal: get up to 5K running intensity for the last 2 intervals without straining madly.

You can also use the pre-set interval sessions on the machine. Be sure they are at the appropriate intensity for your current days requirements and level of fatigue.

Cross training should complement your run training. You need to practice running at 5K and 15K pace (threshold intensity) for the psychomotor perfection of your running form. It is vital to be relaxed at these speeds. Generally, your longer interval sessions should be running.

If you do want to do a full session on the elliptical trainer as a substitute for running once every 2 to 3 weeks...increase the session to 45 minutes and stride elliptically for:

5 times 5 minutes at 85 % of max HR, and 100 strides per minute for threshold training; or

10 times 2 to 3 minutes at 90 to 98 % max HR, at just over 100 strides per minute for VO2 max training.

For the 5-minute repeats, switch direction after 3 minutes. For the 2-minute intervals, switch direction after each interval. You don't have to memorize these sessions. Just switch direction and elevation every 2 to 3 minutes.

There's no point in moving at greater than 100 strides per minute. Even when running at 2-mile race pace you'll be doing less than 100. Increase resistance <u>or</u> incline a bit to get your heartrate up to 98 % of max to work on VO2 max.

Note: 75 percent of your training benefits come from the first half of your interval session. Restricting yourself to fifteen minutes of quality cross training is best for most runners. Save your legs to run productive interval sessions away from machines...though the treadmill has its uses.

Choice Three: The Bicycle

Ride indoors while watching an inspiring video, or outside with the stimulating elements...it depends on how stimulating those elements are.

Bike riding studies show a 9 percent improvement in 10K race times, plus boosts in VO2 max.

In bike riding, the effort is mostly on the thigh muscles, which will help your hill running ability...but without all those risks from ground impact. When biking, the pressure on your joints and bones is less than when walking. In fact, the pressure is less than when merely standing. Because you are working the thighs, biking complements pool running nicely. Point the toes down and you can give the calves a bit of work, but you'll still need to do some calf muscle exercises with weights or against your own body's resistance.

Want to exercise those hamstrings and calves better? Fit toe clips to your pedals so that you can pull up on each revolution. The natural tendency is to simply push down on the pedals, which means the quads do all the work. You'll have to think about pulling the foot up on each revolution until it becomes second nature. You can also use cycling shoes of course, but unless you're riding greater than 50 miles, use the money to replace your running shoes more often. Use your old running shoes for biking.

Biking Regularly can:

* Increase your flexibility because you work running's antagonistic muscles.
* Decrease injuries;
* Improve cadence;
* Make your quadriceps stronger;
* Keep you fit while healing a running injury, especially of the tendons;
* If you have I-T band syndrome, you may want to use a recumbent bike, which reduces the flexion at the hip.

Page 108 stated that you could easily rest while biking downhill. Don't. Peddling at 90 to 100 revolutions with minimal resistance in low gears, or maintaining modest legspeed while free-wheeling will bring nutrients into your muscle cells and get much of the lactic acid from the hill climb out of your muscles. When you start the serious effort again at the base of the hill, your muscle cells will be ready to work.

Inactively sitting on your butt for those downhills will leave your legs stiff, just like when you fail to warmdown after running a track session. You don't have to pedal hard like a professional biker. Maintaining your heartrate at 60 percent of your maximum will keep you in the training zone for the entire ride, instead of only on the flat and uphill.

Use the same rule when approaching red lights. Instead of maintaining hard effort and breaking severely...plan ahead. Coast or spin as you approach the light, and choose your exit gear for carefully getting through the junction.

Specificity rules state that to run well you must train well with mostly running. You practice by running the exact pace you intend to race at, plus a few miles a bit faster to improve VO2 max, and plenty of miles a bit slower for endurance. Yet all three can be achieved with biking. Biking is the third best aerobic cross-training for runners.

Biking lets you amass great training volume, but you need to incorporate some speed riding, and maintain speed running.

You also need to practice the running push off from your toes to work the lower leg muscles, ankle and hamstrings. Maintain your fartlek, threshold pace and interval running, including a few downhill strides to stretch out the hamstrings and gluteal muscles.

Bikers have an easier time with hydration and other fuels. They can carry a ton of liquid on the bike and actually drink it. They can eat carbos with a little protein without being too concerned about it sloshing around in the stomach. An energy bar and 32 ounces of liquid in your belly is no problem on a bike.

Standing on the bike for harsher workouts.

Having someone drive you back down the mountain after hour-long uphills, enable you to stand for most of your riding. Hill climbs allow you to achieve very high heartrates. Maintain good cadence to reduce the strain on the knees. Take an extra shirt to stay warm if you intend to coast back down with occasional spinning of your legs.

Alas, most people sit for the bulk of their bike riding. Sitting is more aerodynamic, but means the heartrate will be 10 percent lower than comparable running workouts.

Twenty to 30 mile rides at 60 percent of max HR twice a week does wonders for a runners endurance. Start by doing these rides instead of a 4 to 6 mile run for a few weeks, then gradually add back the easy run so that your total training volume has increased. Prefer to substitute biking for running? Throw away this page and keep running!

Okay. It takes three to four miles of biking to equal a single mile of running...if you're at appropriate intensity. I believe that biking for twice the time it takes to run a mile is equal to one mile of running. Current easy pace 7:30 per mile? Each quarter of an hour on a bike will give you a running mile equivalent.

Some people will need to organize their life better to find the extra time required for biking instead of running.

When you're comfortable with steady rides, add some threshold pace miles by doing 10 to 15 minutes pretty hard once, twice and then three times in one of your weekly rides. You should feel as if you'd be able to maintain that speed for 40 to 60 minutes. Heartrate should be 75-85 percent of max. Decrease your threshold running sessions the first few weeks while doing these bike intervals.

Working on VO2 max? Two to 5 minute efforts, at a pace you could handle for 15 to 20 minutes would work. Used to 8 x 800 meters at the track? Build toward 8 repeats of one mile on the bike. However, if your biking is in addition to a track session, doing 3 to 4 repeats will give a modest, yet VO2 max enhancing session. This bike session could be the day after your track session, or mere minutes afterwards. Practice good biking form and ride safely.

Four repeats give you about 75 percent of the training benefits of 8 repeats. Short sessions give a disproportionate reward for the effort put in: This half session is a runners best friend...big rewards from modest effort!

Want interval training with friends? Join a spinning class once or twice a week. It's indoors and you'll all be working at your own intensity. Before doing a spinning class however, you should be in good biking shape. You need to be bike fit before you do biking intervals.

Bike buying? Go cheap. In August 2,000 I purchased a mountain bike for $110. Helmet, shorts and sundries, and I was on the road for less than $175. Yes readers...the road. Wide tires with suspension front and back and 21 gears. And a nicely rolling quiet road from my front door.

Like over 90 percent of mountain bikes, it will never experience a trail. I, on the other hand, do experience continuous high quality exercise for 50 to 95 minutes. It's slower than my old 10 speed road bike days, but it's safer at high heartrates because I'm moving slower, and I have a better view of the road or bike path.

Avoiding Bike Pains

Road Burn: Don't fall off your bike or crash into things! Plan ahead for traffic lights, stop signs and the actions of other animals. Break gently as a rule. Find a quiet dirt trail to practice fast stopping, and the art of getting one foot out of your toe clips in a timely manner. Wear safety clothing.

Backache: Distance from seat to handlebars should not stretch your body to discomfort. Ride with your elbows slightly bent and your back at no less than a 50-degree angle to the road. Arch and relax your back every 10 to 15 minutes to reduce muscle fatigue.

Knee pains: Adjust your seat height to get a slight bend at the knee when your foot is at its lowest point. Use easy gears at high cadence instead of straining with big cogs. As in running, keep the knees pointing straight ahead. Keep the patella tracking perfectly or your rides will give you chondromalacia. Push the saddle back if you need to.

Sore butt: Small seat; big seat...err, the one on the bike I mean. Choose the seat which suits you best. Wear biking shorts for the extra cushioning and comfort. Some people say that circulation to the penis can be compromised by squashing the artery and nerves for extended periods. Some bike seats are built up each side to keep the perineal area and vital communication cords safe from most pressure. Don't lean forward onto your perineum for extended periods. Being slim, healthy and fit are all aphrodisiacs.

Stiff neck: Really people, we've moved above the shoulders! Got to see where you're going. Move your head around frequently to reduce neck strain. Mountain bike handlebars are great for runners. Unless you're riding with a fast group, you don't need to ride aerodynamically at 24 miles an hour (mph). You can sit up more, resisting the air at 21 mph. Your legs don't know and can't care.

Tingling hands: Caress rather than grip the handlebars. Change hand positions often. Stretch during breaks. Cruising handlebars are good for long rides.

Walking is good cross-training too.

You can walk for one to two minutes every half an hour during long runs while rehydrating, or you can walk 3 to 5 miles once or twice a week as cross training.

Studies on ground impact during exercise usually take your body weight as the base = 100. Walking scores about 115 compared to running's 250 to 300.

The problem, of course, is getting the heartrate up enough for runners to call it training. Wake up Mr. Paradox! Some of your exercise should be more for relaxation than training. You run easily at 60 to 80 percent of maximum heartrate for 4 to 6 miles for recovery and to maintain or achieve a solid base. Why not walk briskly, and with good form for those 40 to 60 minutes, and relax your way at 50 percent of maximum heartrate. It's possible to maintain 60 percent or more of max HR for 95 % of your walk according to some studies. You'll still burn over 100 calories per mile, and more if it's in deep sand. If walks are in addition to your running, you'll get fitter by building muscles and endurance, and perhaps by losing some weight.

Provided you use good walking technique, ground impact is not much more than when you're standing. Technique is essentially the same as for running, including:

Land with a bent knee;
Gently on the heel;
Roll through the ball of the foot;
Push off with your toes;
Swing the arms back and forward;
Keep your back straight and pull in your abdominals.
Note that race walkers use a straight leg.

The main difference with walking is that there is always at least one foot on the ground. With running, both feet can be off the ground at the same time.

Want quality in your walking? Hills, treadmills, stadium steps, the stairs in high rise buildings or walking in the sand give limitless options for intervals of 2 to 10 minutes at 5K to 15K intensity. Use the elevator instead of walking back down the stairs. Keep the treadmill at zero gradient during recoveries, and you'll never suffer the ground impact of walking downhill. You can also enjoy your walking by avoiding intensity!

Hardly mentioned options.

Cross-country skiing, inline skating or roller bladding are specialty sports which take practice and skill to achieve a decent aerobic workout. Research shows that it is easy to work at 90 percent of your maximum aerobic capacity during the novice stages of these sports: just like with running, you're inefficient in the beginning. With practice, your efficiency improves and your heartrate at a given speed will decrease. However, with experience you will be able to skate or blade for a much longer duration, and significantly increase your aerobic capacity.

The learning curve for a skiing machine is quite rapid. With small snowshoes, snow walking and snow running is an option for many. Hint: Even after the nastiest storms, there is usually running terrain somewhere close by.

Don't go overboard with these exercises. Many are so different to running that you're working a strange group of muscles: fine for cross-training because your running muscles can rest up. Don't strain the other muscles though. Ball sports give negligible aerobic training.

The elliptical sessions can be done on a stair climbing machine, which are easy to use and build quadriceps power. Stairs don't work the arms, and can also cause knee problems. Rowing can actually correct shoulder weaknesses.

Rowing.

Rowing is not in the top three aerobic exercises to suit a runner's needs. However, it is:

* Rhythmic. You can keep going for a considerable time and stimulate the heart and lungs just like with running.
* It works the shoulders. Less than with swimming, but more than during running.

* It works most of the large leg muscles.
* You can enjoy the scenery on the river or lake, though you're more likely to be on a machine.

Every time you push your legs straight in rowing you do a leg-press. The leg-press and squats are ideal weight training exercises because you work the quadriceps, hamstring and buttock muscles. In rowing, you do a leg-press 30 to 40 times every minute for your 10 to 20 minute session.

Moreover, you work the shoulder and arm muscles while giving abdominals and back a goodly bit of work to do. Whether on a rowing machine prior to your elliptical session or out on the water, here's how to row.

* Keep your back nicely arched.
* At full extension of the legs, don't stretch your back out.
* Keep your shoulders back; avoid the tendency to round them forward when extending the arms forward.
* Knees should be in line with your ankles and in line with your hips. Don't bow them in or out.
* Don't lock out. Keep a few degrees of extension in reserve at your elbows and knees.
* Pull yourself back to the bow to work the hamstrings.

Kayaking and canoeing are more focused on the arms than rowing is, so they are poor cross training options.

Your first 10 to 12 weeks at strength and cross training should allow you to rest three times to race. A 5K, 5 miles and 10K would be excellent practice for all runners. Don't rest up very much. Your major peak should be after running a series of Interval sessions at 5K pace, to stimulate your VO2 maximum. The races during your first cross training experience are for training and for personal delight. Then, take your leg muscle and upper body strength into another 20-week half-marathon training program for several more races. Also, make a lifetime commitment to cross training.

Your lungs, heart and the rest of your circulatory system are not too worried about which type of (mainly) aerobic exercise you do. Your mind and your racing ability do need fun exercise and specific exercise respectively. If you find a mix of exercise which is enjoyable, and do about 20 % of it fairly intensely, you'll do it often enough to race well. To become proficient at running, your running must dominate.

The ability to run fast comes from leg muscle strength and oxygen uptake ability. Long steady runs, appropriately paced speed sessions, plus balanced cross training gives you the raw materials to run fast.

Flexibility is also vital. This all-purpose stretch is great during hydration breaks or prior to speed training. Regular stretching and good hydration reduces your risk of cramps.

Chapter Eleven

Racing at 20 miles and 30K

How many reasons do you need to run? If running a marathon is your only goal, simply do a 20 mile training run every other week for three months, plus the rest of your half-marathon training sessions, and get that first (and possibly last) marathon out of the way.

If you can restrain yourself to a four-year plan, spend a year of serious training at the 20 mile and 30K distances. Twenty miles is said to be the half-way point in a marathon. This extra year at 20 mile racing will get you to the half-way point in your first marathon in much better shape than if you hop straight to a marathon schedule. This is a crucial year of training.

That was how this Chapter's first draft started, when it was intended to be part of my Marathon training book. The following pages are adapted to take into account the fact that this chapter is primarily for Half-marathon runners who are ready for the next challenge.

This is another fine opportunity to add mileage. The more miles you run, the stronger your legs will be: Stronger bones, ligaments and tendons, plus stronger muscle fibers which will propel you to stardom with your sub 5 hour or sub 2.5 hour marathon. You will also have the potential to race faster or more comfortable half marathons.

You could replace 2 to 3 miles of distance running with 30 minutes of cross training, but with apologies to the last

40 pages, unless you're running over 40 miles per week, or injury prone, your first choice should be running.

The long run most weeks builds still more stamina into your half-marathon trained body. You will then be able to handle more volume in your threshold pace training sessions, and more repeats in your VO2 max interval sessions, as discussed in Chapters 7 and 8.

If you are going to race well at 20 miles, you need to put in your long runs, decent total mileage, plus a solid volume of quality mileage.

Let's expand on a few things.

* The Long Run this year compared to the Half Marathon.
* Anaerobic pace to race 20 miles & 30K compared to last years half-marathon training.
* Downhill training.
* Other options for improving VO2 maximum.

THE LONG RUN

One purpose of your monthly 22 milers in marathon training is to enhance your muscles' fat burning skills. Burning fatty acids preserves your glycogen supply. Unless you train your muscles to work partially off of fat, you'll run out of glycogen at about the 20-mile point. This point is often called 'The Wall'.

Using fat (fatty acids) as fuel, requires ten percent more oxygen than when burning the sugar, which comes from your glycogen stores.

Simple science dictates that you should slow down by 10 percent when you convert to fat use. It's no coincidence that most runners who hit the wall slow down by 10 percent. Of course, they are also battling muscle fatigue and often dehydration by the 20 mile point. The under trained runner is forced to slow down by more than 10 percent!

Run the first 15 to 20 miles of a marathon at the right pace, and you'll be using a goodly amount of fatty acids for fuel, instead of all of your sugar during the early miles. You will be able to conserve sufficient sugar for those last 6 miles. You will not be forced to slow down...at least not because your fuel supply line has been clogged with fat.

Run plenty of 18s and 20s in training, and at one minute or more per mile slower than target 20-mile race pace, and you'll conserve sugar reserves. Lecture and teach your muscles to become proficient fat burners while running efficiently and you'll have plenty of glycogen to race 20 or more miles.

Racing 20 Miles.

Now, provided you take adequate rest pre-race, and eat sufficient carbohydrates, the wall is still in your future (though perhaps only 100 yards in the future) at the end of a 20-mile race. The 20-mile and 30K races come down to pace judgment, and your medium length long runs.

But medium long distance runs compared to what!

Compared to marathon training, your long runs will be modest. Still only 17 or 18 miles most times; some weeks only 15; occasionally, a 20. The longer runs will be no slower than during half marathon training...one minute per mile slower than race pace. Having graduated from at least a year of half-marathon training, it will only take you a few attempts to get used to a monthly, easy paced 20 mile run.

However, a second change to your long run situation is that you will run part of your 15s a bit faster.

Once you've got used to 20s, every fourth week, or every fourth long run should include 8 to 10 miles within 15 to 30 seconds of your target 20 mile or 30K race pace. This vital session is so close to 20 mile race pace that it will teach your muscle cells to use its fat stores in preference to sugar, and you'll also learn to run economically at a fairly fast pace. The week that you run a fifteen, just like most of your long runs, you will start the run with tired legs. You will be doing it 24 hours after a sensible session of speedwork. It's the combination of sub-maximal days which prepare you for a solid race.

ANAEROBIC THRESHOLD FOR 30K TRAINING

Chapter Seven discusses lactate threshold pace for the half-marathon. You did at least 8 to 10 weeks practicing the art of cruising at 15K pace. Twenty mile and 30K race training allows you to train at the lower levels of threshold pace, closer to 80 percent max heartrate.

Running at 80 percent max HR during half-marathon training would have meant training exactly at race pace. What runners generally look for in speed training is one notch faster than goal race pace. Thus, 15K race pace was the ideal preparation for half-marathons.

For 20 mile and 30K racing however, your threshold pace speedwork can be done at half-marathon pace. The 10 to 15 seconds per mile pace decrease compared to 15K pace makes this running easier, and probably decreases injury risk. You will still be raising your anaerobic threshold limit. Run four to five mile tempo runs at half-marathon pace one week, alternating with long intervals while taking a one to two minute rest.

Or really short rests. In 1998, at age 28, Ronaldo Da Costa took 3 minutes off his marathon personal record, and lopped 45 seconds off of the then world best for the marathon: One of his key sessions was 15 times 1,000 meters at slightly slower than half-marathon pace, barely threshold pace...but with only a 20 to 30 second recovery.

After several sessions of long threshold pace intervals, in which you gradually reduce your rest period, you can increase speed on the last one or two reps. Edge down toward 15K pace for the last mile of a two mile rep, or the last two reps of six times one mile. But don't get carried away. Stay in control, stay at comfortably hard pace. You'll be getting your speed training in the VO2 Max sessions.

Cross-country Training.

You may not have access to cross-country racing, but most runners can train for the cross-country experience. Cross-country running builds the mental character plus the physical strength needed to run long distances. Enter some x-country races, or train as if you were going to race.

Run a series of races or hard runs of 4 to 6 miles, or use long intervals at 15K effort over rough terrain to improve your leg strength. Use dirt, grass and mud sections which give a mile or more of running...over undulating terrain if possible.

Week one...run 4 x one mile
Week two...2 x two miles
Week three...5 x one mile
Week four...2 x three miles
Week five...five miles hard
Week six...5 x one mile
Week seven...resting with 2 x two miles
Week eight...8-mile time trial

The time trial can include low stress U-turns. If your usual loop or section is one mile, stop the watch at the end, jog 15 meters while slowing to do a U-turn, then accelerate and re-start the watch for your return. These 15 seconds will give you a mental breather. When you run these sections as repeats, however, take the one to two minute breaks recommended for normal threshold training.

You can use wind as a training tool.

Run mile repeats into the wind and your cardiovascular system gets a threshold pace workout while your leg muscles amble along at slower than half-marathon pace. Your muscles will be working at threshold effort, but your joints, ligaments and tendons will only get the ground impact of the slower running.

Achieve similar results by running up long gentle slopes. Although you will be running hill repeats most weeks, you can also combine resistance training with threshold pace training to extend or finish this strength phase…by doing long up-hills: Give yourself two types of training in one run to get the maximum value from your miles.

Still More Resistance.

Run hills and other training on the softest surface you can find. Soft surfaces reduce long-term wear and tear on your joints; it reduces bone and muscle injuries. Running is about longevity, not one 20-mile race as preparation for one marathon...prior to retirement from running. Run on soft surfaces for a lifetime of recreation.

Dirt, grass and sand, are better than concrete and asphalt. Seek out mud, snow and grass with a softened base. Top coaches recommend these soft surfaces, which make you work harder for the same speed because:

The surface gives...you work harder at push-off.
You have to lift your feet higher to avoid tripping.
Wet or muddy shoes act like ankle weights.

Downhill Running for Strength.

Yes...for strength. Running strides and repeats on soft surfaces with 1 to 2 percent downgrades work the hamstrings, gluteal muscles, hip flexors and the soleus muscle in the calf. Downhill training will improve your biomechanics, making your running more economic.

The best stride frequency for successful racing is 90 to 95 per minute. Increasing from 90 to 92 per minute can shave 2 minutes from your half-marathon time. Increase your cadence by practicing:

* Short, rapid strides for 30 to 60 seconds.
* Fast leg action with short up-hills.
* Swift strides and repeats down a gentle hill.

Downhills build strength in the hamstring muscles as they pull the lower leg rapidly through during the recovery phase of each stride cycle, and strengthen the gluteal muscles as they extend the hip behind the runner.

Hip extensor muscles include the gluteus maximus muscle and gluteus minimus muscle. Taken together, they are called the gluteal muscles, the gluts, the butt muscles or the glutei muscles. Fast downhill running makes them stronger.

The main hip flexor muscles are the Ilio-soas group (Iliacus muscle and Psoas major muscle), the sartorius and the biceps femoris muscle (or quadricep femoris muscle), one part of the quadriceps muscle. They lift or flex the upper leg--they give us our knee-lift.

If you're warmed up and stretched, proceed to:

Downhill Running to Improve Economy.

The slope should be gentle--one to two percent is sufficient. The surface should be soft: Short grass, fairly even sand or dirt trails, or an old railroad bed, or:
Use a treadmill...if it has the ability.

The First Downhill Sessions.

Just like you would any other form of training, start with gentle strides. The first few sessions must be easy ones to get your muscles used to the faster legspeed, and eventually, an extended stride.

Gravity can speed you to a Doctor and a break from running. Hold back for your early sessions. Keep the stride low and land with a slightly bent knee to act as shock absorbers. Then, instead of pounding down the hill, you'll be easing down them.

* When you're loose...push off with the calf muscles to go faster.
* Make full use of the hip extensor muscles to extend the leg behind you and assist the work of the calf muscles.
* Be conscious of your leg pull-through;
* Whip the leg forward with the hip flexor muscles.
* Think leg speed as you run gently down the slope.
* Work your hamstring muscles to speed the leg through; bring the lower leg closer to your butt than you normally do.
* Do not run so fast that your butt muscles hurt.
* Land softly...midfoot, and roll, then push rapidly off the toes after the support phase.

Run Perpendicular to the Slope.

Leaning forward can strain the gluteal and hamstring muscles. Leaning back puts pressure on the back and hip flexors. You'll be setting up a breaking action. You want a flowing, rhythmic, biomechanically sound running style.

Intermediate Downhill Running.

200 to 400 meter efforts. Short intervals.

Run a modest amount of repeats to begin with--about two thirds of your normal interval session--because you'll be running them faster. You will be close to 2-mile race pace while putting in 5K pace effort.

Think about your running form. Sprinting downhill with arms flying all over the place will not make you a more economical runner.

Push the arms back on each stride, allow them to move straight forward to their natural height; don't grasp for handfuls of air. Hands don't need to go across the chest...unless it's the perfect running form for your body. Straight back and forward to a modest height is best. The arms need to balance the legs: Think RELAXATION.

Advanced Downhill Training.

After three or four sessions of short efforts, move to:

Long Repetitions at VO2 max. 800 to 1,200 meter intervals at 2 mile pace. Actually, you can run 2 mile pace at 5K effort. Running at 2 mile pace is easier than on the flat. Fly during your training. Your heart and lungs will be at 5K pace, but the hip flexors and extensors get the benefit from two mile pace. If you run one out of every four long repeat sessions downhill, your track reps at 5K pace will seem easier...because you will have the legspeed in hand.

A bonus to downhill speedwork is the long rest. Unless you've been driven out to the top of a long grade, or run a four mile warm-up to the top, you have to run back up the hill after each rep. My personal preference is to run one gentle uphill stride at the midpoint of the return journey; it helps to keep me loose, and the muscles warm.

Downhill Running Uses:

* Cruising a few strides is pleasant when you feel tired because you still get to run fast. However, don't substitute downhills for the rest that you may need.
* Race preparation at all distances, because you can run faster than race pace.
* Preparation for downhill races.
* Improved flexibility.

Finally, you can work on running economy without being under as much physiological or lung busting pressure as when you're running on the flat.

Don't want to devote an entire session to downhill running? Former masters champ at the LA and Big Sur Marathons, Greg Horner routinely includes downhill training...when running 2,000 meter repeats, the last 25 percent of it is down a gentle grass slope. Most of the first 1,500 meters is up a 2 to 4 percent grade.

VO2 MAXIMUM STIMULATION.

In 10K & 5K Running & Training, British author Frank Horwill was quoted saying that the best paces to train at to improve VO2 max are 90 to 100 percent of VO2 max, or 10K to 2 mile race pace. While preparing for the half-marathon you used mainly short reps at 5K pace because it:

Gives greater stimulation to your oxygen uptake capacity mechanisms than 10K pace.

With lower injury risk than training at 2 mile race pace.

5K pace training forced you to run economically, teaching your muscles to run fast using less oxygen.

Because of all the miles you are running, and the length of time you have been running high mileage, you should have developed most of your VO2 max potential. Now that your race distance is longer, you can do some of your VO2 max speedwork at 90 percent of VO2 max. It will still:

* Stimulate that little extra improvement in your VO2 max which most runners strive for;
* Force you into economical running for a longer period;
* Give you a sense of satisfaction and confidence in your running ability;
* Because...**you will run very long repeats at 10K pace**.

Unless you run more than 10 percent of your weekly mileage in one session, or use extremely short rests to force your muscles to adapt to a higher level of fatigue, short reps at 10K pace are easy. Marathon champ, Da Costa did take very short rests during his 25 times 400 meters at 10K pace...a 15 to 20 second recovery between reps.

You've done many sessions of short repeats at 5K pace. You could simply shorten your rest breaks while running short reps at 10K pace as Da Costa does. Alternatively, you can stimulate your muscles for longer periods by running longer reps with a short rest. Running 1,200 meters or a mile is not tough at 10K pace, until you follow it with another and another off a fast 200 to 400 meter rest.

Though you've run at least four half-marathons or 20K races, and have more than two years of regular running in the bank, it's prudent to add this 10K pace training gradually. Start with 5 percent of your weekly mileage as a break from short reps at 5K pace. Change a half mile each month until you reach 10 percent of weekly mileage in one session of long reps. Then alternate sessions between short to medium reps at 5K pace with long efforts at 10K pace.

Long reps at 10K pace will give stimulation to your muscles for a greater proportion of the total training time. The same applies to long reps at 5K pace of course. Use a few sessions of long repeats at 5K pace in the early part of your peaking phase.

Doing your VO2 max training at 10K pace instead of 5K pace, and threshold training at half-marathon pace instead of 15K pace will leave your legs nice and fresh for a 20 mile run, or those 8 to 10 miles at close to 20 mile race pace during one of your other long runs.

Use all the above forms of training for 20 mile racing. The long run is only two miles longer than when training for the half-marathon. Your threshold pace running is closer to 80 percent max HR, or about 10 seconds per mile slower than when half-marathon training. Half of your VO2 max training can be at 10K pace: again, 10 to 15 seconds slower than during your half-marathon training. This combination should leave you fresh enough to add more mileage or cross training.

This may be the perfect chance to move from the 40 mile per week to a 50 mile per week schedule...by adding 2 miles per month. Or, because you now find the running is easier, you could increase the volume of your speed sessions by half a mile each month. Or, you could add a solid 60 minute cross training session doing 30 minutes of weight training, then 30 minutes on an elliptical trainer, bicycle or in the pool. Make the combination of changes that work for you.

Belong to a gym? Cross training will be easy to add. No desire to exercise indoors, but sick of your work place? A lunchtime five mile run, on what would otherwise be a rest day, works well. Still only want to run four days a week? Adding an extra mile to each speed session would be a good candidate.

Slot each type of distance training in to your program, based on the percentage which that element should be. When doing 80 miles per week, you should be able to handle 8 times a one-mile repeat at anaerobic threshold pace. If your body only allows you 80 miles every two weeks, four times a one mile repeat one week, alternating with a four mile tempo run the next week will do you good. Do the aerobic stuff for your mitochondria and red blood cell production too.

You may recall from the weight training section that you get 75 percent of the strength benefits from one set of weight training that you get from three sets. You also get 75 percent of the running benefits from the first half of a speed session. If you don't feel like running, but get yourself out anyway and run one mile at 10K pace, then 4 x 400 at 5K pace, you'll get most of the training benefits from the full session. Many times though, you'll just continue and run close to a full training session! If not, you will still feel better about yourself because you got out there, yet you'll be pleasantly rested for your next run.

A gentle fartlek session is another option on "don't feel like training, or bad weather days." Clothe yourself appropriately and run some striders on a soft surface for ten minutes. As you cruise through the striders you'll probably come up with a minimum acceptable session concept of say two times 5 minutes at 15K effort. Finish with some more striders and you will have trained on what could have been a wasted day.

The Training Schedule incorporating long repeats at 10K pace is on page 161. In only two weeks out of every five does your long run differ from your half-marathon training in earlier Chapters. Fast 9 actually means 3 miles at 70 percent max HR to warm up, then 9 miles at close to 20 mile race pace (run about 30 seconds slower than current half-marathon pace), and then a three mile warmdown.

The slower pace for half of your speed sessions is the other major change, and allows you to add five to ten miles per week to reach 50 to 55 miles for most weeks. Quality cross-training sessions are fine if you prefer not to add running mileage. Remember that just like last year, the Day Four session in the first three weeks is usually within the context of a 12-mile run. You get three reasonably harsh training weeks and two remarkably easy weeks per rotation.

After going 4 to 6 times through this 5 week schedule, rest up like you did for your half-marathon, and race at 30K or 20 miles. During the next six months race a half-marathon, plus a few 10Ks and 5Ks, and then another 20 mile race. Use this second six months to work on weaknesses.

	Day One	Two	Three	Four
Probably	*Sat*	*Sun*	*Tues*	*Thurs*
Wk 1	H 12 x 400	18	V@5K	T5
2	V@10K	20	H 8 x 600	CI 5
3	H 16 x 200	Fast 9	V@5K	T5
4	V@10K	12	CI3	F 3.0
5	Race at 10K to ten miles.			

If the race was 10 miles, this fifth week is for recovery, but because your focus is a 20 mile or 30K race, you should probably run an easy fifteen miler three days after the race. A very gentle session of striders at 5K pace would be prudent on the Thursday, and set you up to repeat the first four weeks.

T = Tempo runs are usually at half-marathon pace this year. Run 2 mile repeats if you prefer.

CI = Cruise intervals: do only 25 percent of them at 15K pace; do the rest at half marathon pace, but with short recoveries.

H = Hills: 3 sessions per 5 weeks, including two sessions within 4 days. Some of you may prefer a hilly fartlek session on soft terrain.

F = Fartlek...do mostly short efforts at 5K effort but mix in a couple long efforts at 15K pace.

V@10K = Long reps at 90 percent VO2 max (10K pace).

V@5K = The variety of shorter intervals at 5K pace, just like you did for half-marathon training in Chapter Eight.

During each 10 week training cycle, you could consider these four sessions at 10K race pace.

* 1,200 meters with a 200 meter rest;
* Miles with a 400 rest;
* 2,000s with a 400 rest;
* 2-mile reps with an 800 rest.

The quantity of reps will be about 10 % of your weekly mileage. Even though you routinely race 10Ks, ease up to 10 % of mileage at 10K race pace over several sessions.

Run okay at 15K and 5K paces for long and short reps respectfully, but find those 10K reps to be a beast? You should, because running long repeats at 10K pace with a short rest is tough. That is part of the reason they are so good for you; they stimulate your physiological systems.

Beginning to dread them? Try running 800s with two minutes of fast jogging for rest, instead of the 1,200s. Run miles instead of 2,000s. Break up a session of 1,000s by running five times 300 meters at 5K pace at the half-way point in your session. Make the sessions palatable to you, or entertaining to your training partners.

Then go back to running the longer repeats to give greater stimulation to your muscles' systems. The first lap of any repeat is easy. Run 5 laps (2,000 meters), and you'll get 33 percent more of your training in the stimulating or more difficult zone, compared to running 4 laps per repetition. Four times 2,000 meters is much more stimulating and therefore more beneficial than 5 x 1,600.

Now, before showing you the detailed half marathon training schedules, lets add a few comments on warm-ups.

Jump straight into Interval sessions and you'll produce stress hormones, making you prone to illness. Not good.

Warm-ups, that is, low intensity exercise before your main bout of training may help prevent colds and flu by protecting your immune system. Warming up also lowers blood pressure, sets up improved blood flow to the heart and other muscles, reduces injury risk, makes your perceived effort seem easier, thus allowing you to run longer or at higher heartrates depending on your goal today!

Chapter Twelve

20 to 60 week schedules at 30 to 40 miles per week.

Be half-marathon ready in 20 weeks or 60 weeks depending upon your experience. The schedules are split into three degrees of commitment:

* Serious runners who run fast once a week;
* Moderately intensive trainers with two speed sessions;
* High intensity runners with three speed running days each week.
* 30 mile per week runners will rest two days and cross train on two days each week. Their three running days are mapped out on pages 171-172. The long run is shorter than 40 per week people. You could run Sunday, Tuesday & Thursday, so your typical week would be 14, 8 and 8 miles with 3 to 4 miles of it at speed just like the 40 miles per week people.

Phase One: Base Mileage.

Your true base was achieved with the two or more years which you ran while racing at 5K to 10 miles. Now the big question is, how long should your long run be when cruising through the third year of half marathon training, while running forty miles per week?

The 40 percent rule for your longest run gives you a 16 miler, plenty enough for the half marathon! Run it at only 60 percent of your maximum heartrate, or these runs will be too grueling.

This leaves you 24 miles that you can split between 3 additional runs. Fewer, but longer runs give you more endurance than many short runs. At least one run should be 4 miles of fartlek as described in Chapter Three.

Very experienced runners may need only 4 weeks in this fartlek phase, and be ready for another half marathon in 20 weeks. If you're entering year 3 of half marathon training for the first time, you may need 10 to 16 weeks of fartlek while building toward those 16-mile runs. Move to Phase Two when you're ready; you'll take 50 to 60 weeks to be truly half marathon ready.

Schedule for moderately intense runners.

Day 1: Usually Sunday. Long, gentle run. Add a half-mile each week until you can alternate 13, 15 and 17s.

Days 2, 4 and 6 are rest days for a walk or 40 to 60 minutes of gentle cross training.

Day 3: 7 miles--include some fartlek of various lengths and at 5K to 15K pace intensity.

Day 5: 8 miles easy, but ease up toward 75 percent of maximum heartrate for 2 to 3 miles of it.

Day 7: 7 to 9 miles, including 4 miles of more intense fartlek than Day Three. Make it count, but run no faster than 5K race pace in the speedy sections because you'll be running long tomorrow. Run with good form.

Phase Two: Hills and Strength.

Chapter Three had you running hills in step one of half-marathon training, building up the number of hill repeats concurrently while increasing the volume of fartlek running.

However, this 5-phase program separates the types of training somewhat. Hilly fartlek sessions will rejoin phase one and two into one step. The goal is still the same: Build up leg strength while also running at speed each week; use the system which suits you best.

The number of hills or speed training days dictates how seriously you take half-marathon running...or how fast your body recovers from training to allow you to run hard again.

Serious trainers are running fast once a week to enhance running form and stimulate oxygen uptake systems as described in prior chapters. They can alternate hill repeats with their fartlek session each week, giving one hill session every two weeks or once every 8 runs.

The highest intensity runners will train fast three times a week, and add the hill session every week to their fartlek.

This chapter summarizes the moderately intense runners, who enjoy two speed sessions per week. Every week you'll get one session each of hills and fartlek.

Do take care of your Achilles during hill training. You should have done hills many times before, but increase the number of repeats sensibly, and run no faster than 2 mile race pace effort. No collapsing at the end of each repeat! Include some bounding, jumps and striders each week too (see page 37).

The long runs remain the cornerstone of your aerobic endurance, teaching you to run economically even better than your speed running does. Strength and aerobic cross training should be progressing nicely on two of those non-running days.

Provided you've been here before, and routinely run hills at all stages of your training, 4 weeks will again suffice to achieve the 20-week half marathon plan. Achieving the full rewards from hill training and mileage can take half a year of regular hill repeats! Ten sessions should give you 90 percent of this years potential.

Moderately intense runners.

Day 1: Long and gentle. Continue to rotate 13, 15 and 17s, or up to 2.5 hours of running. Increase pace toward 70 percent of maximum heartrate for the last 5 miles.
Days 2 and 4 are restive cross training. Take a complete rest on Day Six.
Day 3: 7 miles--do two miles of hill repeats. Alternate long repeats one week with steeper, but short hills the next week.
Day 5: 8 miles easy, but ease up toward 80 percent of maximum heartrate for a couple of miles.
Day 7: 7-9 miles with 4 miles of intense fartlek. This should feel no harsher than the hill session!

Phase Three: Anaerobic Threshold Running.

15K pace running is another key to your half marathon strength endurance. 15K pace is easier to run than 10K pace, yet it's more beneficial because:

* It stimulates your anaerobic threshold to rise...allowing you to maintain higher race paces for a long time.
* Forces you to run economically and concentrate on running form.
* But...leaves your legs rested for other speed training.

The serious half-marathon trainer who runs fast once a week replaces the hills or fartlek with one quality threshold pace session per week for 6 weeks. Or they could alternate a hilly fartlek run with threshold pace for 8-10 weeks.

Moderately intense heroes who run fast twice a week alternate fartlek with hills on Day Three, and run threshold pace on Day Seven. Switch these days if you wish.

Our highest intensity heroines will run one session every week of fartlek, hills and threshold pace...while maintaining the ever-present long run.

For all of you, injury prevention guidelines allow 10 percent of your mileage to be 15K pace, or four miles. Eight times half a mile with a 30 second rest; 4 x one mile with 60 seconds rest; 2 x two miles; and a continuous 4-mile run, give a nice four-week rotation. Start at 80 percent of maximum heartrate and increase pace to 85 or 90 percent. You should start these sessions at about half-marathon pace, and end up 10 to 15 seconds per mile slower than your best recent 10K pace. The speed table is on pages 202-203.

No races at 10K or 10 miles locally which fit into your race preparation? You can double your anaerobic session once a month instead of racing. Eight times one mile at 10 mile pace with a one minute rest is much easier than a 10 mile race...provided you rest up for it with your low mileage week. However, most areas have a race at 10K to the half-marathon every 3 to 8 weeks. Rest up for them.

Going longer than 6 weeks without a race of more than 5K? Do the big threshold pace session instead of a race. It is 20 percent of your weekly mileage, but that's much less than a long race would be!

Most runners should also do a 5K race once a month for:

* The joy of it...cruising at high speed with no expectation of personal records because you didn't rest up to race.
* Socialization with numerous runners.
* A pleasant break from hill or threshold training sessions.

Moderately intense runners.

Day 1: Long and gentle run. Continue to rotate 13, 15 and 17s. Increase pace toward 70 percent of maximum HR for the second half of each run.

Days 2, 4 and 6 are unchanged.

Day 3: 7 miles: Alternate

A: Two miles of hill repeats. Alternate long and short hills.

B: 4 miles of intense but relaxed fartlek.

Day 5: 8 miles easy, and ease back to 75 percent of maximum heartrate for your fast section because on...

Day 7: 7 to 9 miles with 4 miles at threshold pace.

Phase Four: VO2 Maximum Training.

Running at 2-mile race pace to 5K pace adds power to your muscle fibers and improves the amount of oxygen you can process...and therefore your speed potential. As always, you have several options.

Serious trainers will replace the threshold pace running, which had been a hill session, which had been a fartlek session, with the VO2 pace Intervals.

The moderately hard trainer can rotate hills, hilly fartlek and threshold running on Day Three, while running a series of VO2 max Intervals on Day Seven for 6-12 weeks.

The highest intensity 40 mile per week person can also do the VO2 sessions on Day Seven, but will run two quality mid-week on Days 3 and 5 (perhaps Tuesday and Thursday) such as:

Week One: Hills followed by threshold.
Week Two: Threshold followed by fartlek.
Week Three: Fartlek followed by hills.

The fourth week only needs one midweek quality run of hilly fartlek, which includes a few long reps at threshold pace...to rest up for a long race at the weekend. Don't rest up for 5K races. 5K races substitute for interval sessions once a month, and for the reasons outlined on page 167.

The VO2 Intervals will progress from 3 to 4 miles as described in Chapter Eight, but add long reps at 10K pace once a month. Keep doing your 6,000 meters to 4 miles of intervals at 5K to 10K paces until you have no serious muscle aches afterwards. You'll probably need to run each full session three times for your muscle fibers to fully adapt, and to teach yourself to relax and run economically. The Interval speed table is on page 205.

Surprise, surprise, the long run is unchanged during Phase Four, because you're still developing endurance and running efficiency.

Remember you 30 mile per week runners: Restrict yourself to about 14 miles for your long run, and restrict speed sessions plus their warm-ups to total 8. And cross train.

Phase Five: Half-Marathon Peaking.

Rest and longer repeats at 2 mile to 10K race pace combine to give extra pep to your legs and maximize your VO2 capacity.

The serious trainer replaces short Intervals with three sessions each of 800 and 1,200 meter repeats at 5K pace. The last session 4 days pre-race could be a modest 10 x 300 meters at 5K pace, or 2 x one mile at 15K pace.

The moderately intense runner will reduce his or her midweek session of hills, or threshold, or fartlek to 2.5 to 3 miles of speed running in order to be fresh for the Day Seven long repeats.

Highest intensity runners can run three miles of short Intervals at 5K pace for relaxation midweek, followed by a shorter session of hills or threshold running the next day, or two days later. These highly experienced runners may run mile repeats at close to 2-mile race pace on two of the six weekends leading into their race; they may also be content with the 800s and 1,200s. Most weeks, 5K pace is fast enough for these long repeats.

Most of you can reduce the two midweek runs by one mile for the first two weeks of the 7 leading into the race, by two miles for the next two weeks, and by three for the penultimate two weeks. Mileage decreases to 34.

The next to last ingredient is your long run. Over the last six weeks, try 13, 15, 17, 15, 13 and then a 10 the weekend before the race. The last 17 is four weeks pre-race, so you your body will have plenty of time to recover and make its physiological adaptations inspired by that run!

Thirty mile per week runners decrease their runs in the last three weeks to reach 25 per week.

Note: Don't run the final 10 miler any faster than your usual long run pace: you're supposed to be resting up. Choose a flat course instead of a hilly course.

The last week will include those 300s, and a five mile run to give you 22 miles for the week. If preceded by several 32 to 36 mile weeks and decreasing length of long runs, you'll be nicely rested for the half-marathon.

Training table abbreviations:
E = Easy runs...at 60-70 percent of maximum heartrate.
F = Fartlek
H = Hill repeats
HF = Hilly fartlek...a bit less vigorous than the hill session.
A = Anaerobic threshold pace running...15K speed.
V = VO2 maximum pace intervals...2 mile to 5K speed.
All types of quality running require a warm-up and cooldown of two to three miles. As you'll be doing 4 miles at speed (or 2 miles for hill training), most speed days are about 8 miles.

Serious Runners at 40 miles per week move their legs fast once a week, but can also run two times one mile at half marathon pace during each 15 mile run. Don't do the long repeats at VO2 maximum the first time through. Instead, spend an extra six weeks with 600s and 400s, learning the art of fast running while using very little energy.

Day	One	Three	Five	Seven
Perhaps...	*Sun*	*Tu*	*Thurs*	*Sat*
Weeks 1 to 10	14	8E	4F	8E
Weeks 11, 14, 17	13	8E	2H	8E
Weeks 12, 15, 18	15	8E	2H	8E
Weeks 13, 16, 19	17	6E	4HF	7E
Week 20	12	6E	2HF	Race 10K
Weeks 21, 24, 27	13	8E	4HF	8E
Weeks 22, 25, 28	15	7E	4A	8E
Weeks 23, 26, 29	17	6E	4A	7E

Probably...	*Sun*	*Tu*	*Thurs*	*Saturday*
Week 30	10	6E	2HF	Race 10 miles
Week 31	5E	6E	3HF	8E
Weeks 34, 37	13	8E	4HF	8E
Weeks 32, 35, 38	15	7E	4V	8E
Weeks 33, 36, 39	17	6E	4V	7E
Week 40	10	6E	2HF	Race 10K

Then practice long repeats at 5K to 10K race paces for six weeks, but include your 17-mile run halfway through.

Week 41	13	8E	4V	8E
Week 42	15	7E	4V	7E
Week 43	17	6E	4HF	6E
Week 44	15	7E	4V	8E
Week 45	13	6E	3V	6E
Week 46	10	4E	2V	4E

Then race your half marathon.

The drawback to using training phases is that you can lose the benefit from one type of training while perfecting the next type. Example: no more hills are scheduled after week 19. You can maintain your leg strength and knee lift by doing hilly fartlek, and by running one in three of your threshold sessions up a gentle hill of 2 to 4 percent grade. During the VO2 maximum phase, include a few hilly fartlek sessions with half of it being long efforts at threshold intensity. Cross train also on Monday and Wednesday.

With the 30 mile per week option, runners also move their legs fast once a week, and should run two times one mile at half marathon pace during each 12 mile run. Long repeats at VO2 maximum are useful but you could spend an extra six weeks with 600s and 400s, learning the art of fast running while using very little energy, and using as little oxygen as possible.

Day Or...	Sat Sun	Mon Tues	Wed Thurs	*Races on Sat or Sun*
Weeks 1 to 10	12	8E	4F	
Weeks 11, 14, 17	12	8E	2H	
Weeks 12, 15, 18	13	8E	2H	
Weeks 13, 16, 19	14	6E	4HF	
Week 20	10	6E	2HF	Race 10K
Weeks 21, 24, 27	12	8E	4HF	
Weeks 22, 25, 28	13	7E	4A	
Weeks 23, 26, 29	14	6E	4A	
Week 30	10	6E	2HF	Race 10 miles
Week 31	Rest	6E	2HF	
Weeks 34, 37	12	8E	4HF	
Weeks 32, 35, 38	13	7E	4V	or 5K race
Weeks 33, 36, 39	14	6E	4V	
Week 40	10	6E	2HF	Race 10K
Practice long repeats at 5K to 10K race paces for six weeks.				
Week 41	12	8E	4V	
Week 42	13	7E	4V	
Week 43	14	6E	4HF	
Week 44	13	7E	4V	or 5K race
Week 45	12	6E	3V	
Week 46	10	4E	2V	

Then, race the half marathon. Cross train twice a week for the first 40 weeks. Do one gentle cross training session in weeks 20, 30, 41 to 45 or any week leading into a 10K race.

<u>Moderate Intensity Runners</u> move their legs fast twice a week, and like serious runners, should also run two times one mile at half marathon pace during each 15 mile run, but also in some of their 17 mile runs. You can spend the final 6 weeks running long repeats at close to VO2 maximum or 2-mile to 10K pace the first time through this schedule. Do keep speed running relaxed at all times.

Very experienced at running? Decrease the fartlek and anaerobic sections to 4 and 6 weeks. The fartlek section is often the recovery from a 10-mile to half marathon race. If so, 12s would be sufficient for your long runs. To turn this 40 mpw schedule into an 11-week program, do two weeks in each phase, and alternate 17s & 14s for your long runs. Your 11th week would be the same as the 46th week below.

Strength is vital for running, so reducing the hill section is short sighted. Continue the hilly fartlek and weight training during VO2 max phases to retain muscle strength. No weights in weeks 45 or 46 or the week before a 10K.

Day	One	Three	Five	Seven	
Probably...	*Sun*	*Tu*	*Thurs*	*Sat*	
Weeks 1, 3...9	15	4F	8E	4F	
Weeks 2, 4...10	13	4F	6E	4HF	
Weeks 11, 14, 17	13	4F	8E	2H	
Weeks 12, 15, 18	15	4F	8E	2H	
Weeks 13, 16, 19	17	3HF	7E	2H	
Week 20	12	3HF	5E	Race 10K	
Weeks 21, 24, 27	13	4F	8E	4A	
Weeks 22, 25, 28	15	2H	7E	4A	
Weeks 23, 26, 29	17	3HF	6E	4A	
Week 30	10	3HF	5E	Race 10 mile	
Week 31	6E	8E	3HF	3V	
Weeks 34, 37	13	4HF	8E	4V	
Weeks 32, 35, 38	15	2H	7E	3V	
Weeks 33, 36, 39	17	4A	6E	4V	
Week 40	10	3A	5E	Race 10K	
Then practice long repeats at 5K pace for six weeks.					
Week 41	13	4HF	8E	4V	
Week 42	15	2H	7E	3V	
Week 43	17	3HF	6E	4V	
Week 44	15	4A	7E	4V	
Week 45	13	3HF	6E	3V	
Week 46	10	2V	2A	4E	Race

<u>Highest Intensity Runners</u> shift rapidly for part of nearly every run. Most people doing three quality runs will run more than 40 miles per week, but thousands find 40 to be the ideal level for their running. Two miles of half marathon pace practice is still useful during some of your 13 to 17 mile runs. Your other days are something like this:

Day	One	Three	Five	Seven
Probably...	*Sun*	*Tu*	*Thurs*	*Sat*
Weeks 1 & 3	15	4F	4HF	4F
Weeks 2 & 4	13	4F	4HF	4F
Weeks 5, 8, 11	13	4F	4HF	2H
Weeks 6, 9, 12	15	4F	4HF	2H
Weeks 7, 10, 13	17	3F	3HF	2H
Week 14	12	3HF	2F	Race
Weeks 15 & 18	13	4F	2H	4A
Weeks 16 & 19	15	2H	4HF	4A
Weeks 17 & 20	17	3HF	2H	4A
Week 21	12	2HF	2A	Race
Weeks 22 & 25	13	4HF	2H	4V
Weeks 23 & 26	15	2H	4A	3V
Weeks 24 & 27	17	3HF	4A	4V
Week 28	10	3A	1F	Race
Week 29	5E	2F	3HF	4V
Week 30	14	2H	4V	4V
Week 31	16	2H	4A	4V
Week 32	17	3HF	4A	4V
Week 33	14	4V	2H	4V
Week 34	13	3HF	3A	3V
Week 35	10	2V	2A	4E Race your half marathon.

Note: weeks 30 & 33 contain two 4-mile sessions working on VO2 max. The midweek session is usually short reps at 2-mile pace. The weekend session long repeats at 5K to 10K pace. Longer and close to 10K pace is probably best.

Finally. All runners at 30 to 40 miles per week will benefit from two cross training sessions per week of weights followed by a cardiovascular activity.

Peaking for your race requires reduced mileage and cross training to allow your muscle cells to adapt while resting up. Usually lift 40 pounds for 16 repeats on 12 different exercise machines? Decrease to 30 pounds for 12 repeats the penultimate two weeks and put your muscles through a full range of motion. Bike at 20 mph for 75 minutes twice a week? Slow down to 18 miles per hour...and ride for 50 minutes. Do no cross training in the last week prior to the most significant race of your year.

As one of my favorite cartoons from Running Dialogue *says: "Drink and rest copiously leading into races." Replace most of the liquids which you lose within half an hour of losing it. Running longer than 45 minutes? Replace some of the liquids plus a bit of sugar while running.*

Chapter Thirteen

A 10 to 20 week Half - Marathon program which Averages 40 miles per week.

Adapted from the author's web site at www.runningbook.com

Consistency is the key to half marathon training success. Ignoring the last week, your mileage varies from 35 to 44 for a total of nearly 800 over the 20 weeks. You'll make subtle changes to your training from week to week and over the nearly 5 months to your race.

There is only one assumption for this schedule: You should have trained at 30 to 40 miles per week while racing 5K and 10Ks for at least 6 months. If not, then check the half-marathon training advice in Chapters 3, 7 & 8 to give yourself the fundamentals before embarking on this short-cut half-marathon program.

Training table abbreviations:

E = Easy running at 60-70 percent of your maximum heartrate

X = Cross training such as an hour of bicycle riding, a brisk walk, weight training, or 30 minutes of pool running.

F = Fartlek or speedplay. See Chapter Three for details.

H = Hills. Also, See Chapter Three.

R = Rest

A = Anaerobic threshold pace running...15K race pace. Details in Chapter Seven. Speed table pages 202-203.
V = Interval training at VO2 maximum or 10K to two mile race pace. See Chapter Eight and page 157. Speed table pages 204-205.
All types of speed running require a warmup, stretching and a cooldown. For example, F4 means a 2-mile warmup, 4 miles of fartlek, followed by running a two mile warmdown.

Day	Sat	Sun	M	Tu	W	Th	*Weeks*
Day #	*1*	*2*	*3*	*4*	*5*	*6*	*Mileage*
Week # 1	F4	E12	X	F4	E4	E8	40
Two	A4	E14	X	F4	X	E10	40
Three	H2	E13	X	F4	X	E10	38
Four	H2	E16	X	F4	X	E10	41
Five	A4	E14	X	H2	X	E10	39
Six	F4	E15	X	H2	X	E10	40
Seven	A4	E14	X	F3	R	E8	37
Eight	10K Race	E12	X	F4	X	E10	40
Nine	A4	E18	X	H2	X	E10	43
Ten	V4	E15	X	H2	X	E10	40
Wk 11	V4	E15	X	F4	E5	E8	44
12	H2	E13	X	A4	R	E8	35
13	15K Race	E8	X	F4	X	E10	39
14	V4	E18	X	H2	X	E10	42
15	A5	E14	X	V4	R	E7	38
16	10K Race	X	E5	E8	X	F4	38
17	H2	E15	X	V4	X	E10	40
18	A4	E18	X	F4	X	E8	42
19	V4	E14	R	A4	X	E7	37
20	V3	E11	R	E3	A2	E3	30

It's arbitrary, but day one is Saturday. Friday of course is always for rest.

Note that 6 of the 9 hill training sessions are in the first 10 weeks, yet you maintain strength because the ninth hill session is in week 17.

VO2 max training and those 3 long runs dominate the 10 weeks leading toward your half marathon. Both will teach you to run economically. Except for the last week, any VO2 max session can be replaced by a 5K race. Limit yourself to 2 races at 5K though.

Fartlek training should be of high quality in the early weeks. In the second 10 weeks, use fartlek running mainly as recovery from races and the longer runs: run it less intensely.

The race in week 8 should probably be a 10K. You rest up for it.

In week 13, a 15K or 10 mile race is ideal. If your goal is a 20-mile race, then a half marathon race would be fine for week 13. Run the first 5 miles at 10 seconds per mile slower than even pace for your current half marathon speed.

You do not rest up much for the week 16 race. A 10K would be perfect and make it count by running hard. No race close by? Run 8 times one mile at half marathon pace, followed by 2 times one mile at 10K pace. You did rest up for this day didn't you?

Less than 800 miles to a decent half marathon.
This modest mileage program is for experienced runners at the shorter distances. This author believes that all long distance racers should experience shorter races first.

You could add 2 miles to two of your steady runs each week, plus a mile to one of your speed sessions each week to give yourself an average of 45 miles per week. You could also repeat a three week section several times to give yourself a 30-week preparation. The options are endless, so please adapt it to suit your needs.

Do enough training in your weak areas to achieve improvement, but also retain some training in your strong areas because after all, they are your strengths, and you probably find them more enjoyable.

Runners are apt to do their long runs too fast, sprint up hills, run threshold at 10K pace by mistake, and do intervals at close to mile speed or faster. Try not to make any of those four errors.

* Feel wiped out after your long runs? Slow down and run at less than 70 percent of max heartrate. Run slower than 8 minutes per mile. Take a one-minute walk break every mile.
* Hills hurting you? Run at 2 mile to 5K intensity for 60 to 90 seconds and do not sprint.
* Hate threshold sessions because you hurt for ages? Slow down to 15K pace.
* Interval training feel hard? Slow down to 5K pace and it should feel relatively easy. Still too hard? Reduce the number of repeats until your body can handle it, then increase by a quarter mile every other week until you get back up to 4 miles at speed per session.

Fit enough to start at week 11? You'll have a 10-week half-marathon program. However, consider using the longer build up here or those in Chapter Twelve.

Race time prediction is covered on page 107. This chapters schedule was adapted from the author's "marathon in 20 weeks program", so lets add to page 107 that:

If you expect to run well at the marathon, 20 seconds per mile slower than 10K pace is a reasonable goal for the 6 to 7 minute mile runner at the 20K and half-marathon. The closer you run to your 10K pace when racing a half-marathon, the greater is your aerobic and anaerobic endurance, and your potential at the marathon.

Chapter Fourteen

Training schedules at 50 and 60 miles per week.

Most of this Chapter's narrative is similar to Chapter 12 because it gives you a book summary.

Very experienced half-marathon runners can concentrate on one aspect of their running for 10 weeks, and be race ready in 16 weeks. That is, 3 weeks of recovery running from the prior race, 10 weeks working on a weak point, followed by a 3 week taper.

Moderately experienced runners will need 20 to 40 weeks to get ready for another half marathon, and race several 5K and 10Ks en-route. Some of you have prepared for half marathons at 40 to 45 miles per week, so you'll need 30 weeks or more to get used to the higher mileage. Some of you have raced 10Ks at 50 to 60 miles per week, so you'll need 20 weeks or more to adapt to the longer runs.

As usual, there are serious runners who run fast once a week, moderately intensive trainers with two speed sessions, and, high intensity runners with three speed running days each week.

<u>Fifty mile per week runners</u> have many options in using their extra 10 miles compared to 40 miles per week runners:

* Add a mile or two to all four runs, plus run a four to five mile run to the complete the 50.
* Add the extra mile to the cooldown during quality days.

* Alternatively, add that extra mile as speedwork.
* When moving from 40 to 50 miles per week, add only 2 miles per week.

Running more than 17 or 18 miles in one run does little to improve your half marathon...provided you race half-a-dozen times per year at 10 miles or more. Running closer to 18 miles on your shorter weekends will improve your potential. While rotating 13, 15 and 17s at 40 miles per week, you had an average long run of 15 miles. Sneaking in a couple of 18s instead of 13s every 10 weeks will take your average long run to 16 miles! An 18 is merely 36 percent of your weekly mileage, so it's easier to recover from than a 17 was at 40 per week. Keep it slow to avoid taxing yourself.

Adding to your 4 miles of fast running needs great care. Starting the first few repeats at appropriate pace is even more vital than in prior years. Add a quarter mile every two weeks to reach your 5-mile speed running sessions. Two or three 5 mile sessions at the end of each 6 to 10 week phase should be enough the first time you train for a half marathon at 50 miles per week.

The next time through this schedule at 50 per week, run the entire phase with 5-mile sessions, and increase pace slightly from half-marathon to 15K pace in Phase Three, and from 5K to 2 mile race speed during most of Phase Four and Peaking. Include long reps at 10K pace too.

Hill training edges up to 2.5 miles of repeats. Try even more on the days that they are up a long gentle incline because you'll be at threshold effort instead of 5K intensity.

Half of your bonus 10 miles should probably be done on one of your rest days. Run just before your 30-minute weight training session as the warm-up, or 8 to 10 hours before it as a separate session if that works better for you.

The 5 essential elements of half marathon training are unchanged from the 40 miles per week schedule.

Phase One: Base Mileage.

You have an excellent base from three years of training and racing at 5K to perhaps the 20 miles. The average length of your long run will increase by a mile compared to the 40 mile per week schedule while you cruise through this graduate school year at fifty miles per week.

Split your remaining 32 to 37 miles between 4 additional runs. Fewer, but longer runs give you more endurance than many short runs. At least one run should be 5 miles of fartlek as described in Chapter Three.

Very experienced runners may need only 2 to 4 weeks in this fartlek phase, and be ready for another Half marathon in 10 weeks. If you're entering year 4 for the first time, you may need 8 to 10 weeks of fartlek running while building toward regular 18-mile runs.

Moderately intense runners.

Day 1: Long, gentle run. Bring in 18s.
Day 2: Recovery 5-mile run, plus 40 minutes cross training.
Day 3: 8 miles, with 5 miles of gentle fartlek.
Day 4: 40 to 60 minutes of cross training.
Day 5: 10 miles easy, but ease up toward 75 percent of maximum HR for 2 to 3 miles of it.
Day 6: Rest.
Day 7: 9 miles, including 5 miles of intense fartlek. Make it count, but no faster than 5K pace. Run with good form.

Phase Two: Hills and Strength.

The number of hills or speedy days dictates how intense your running is...or how rapidly your body recovers from training.

Serious runners are training fast once a week to enhance running form and to stimulate oxygen uptake systems. They can alternate hill repeats with their fartlek session each week, giving one hill session every two weeks or once every 10 runs. They should also run 16 times about 100 meter striders on grass each week to improve running form.

The highest intensity runners train fast three times a week, adding the hill session every week to the two fartlek sessions.

Take care of your Achilles' during hill training. Increase the number of repeats sensibly, and run no faster than 2 mile pace effort. No collapsing at the end of each hill repeat!

Long runs are the key to your aerobic endurance. Strength training should be progressing on two easy days.

Provided you've been here before, and routinely run hills at all stages of your training, 4 weeks will suffice to achieve the 20-week half marathon plan. Achieving the full rewards from hill training and mileage can take half a year of regular hill repeats! Ten sessions should give you 90 percent of this year's potential on the fifty-week plan.

Moderately intense runners:

* Will increase pace toward 70 percent of maximum heartrate for the last 5 miles of each long run.
* Run 2.5 miles of hill repeats on Day 3. Alternate long repeats one week with steeper, but shorter hills the next week.
* Ease up toward 80 percent of maximum HR for a couple of miles on Day 5.
* Continue Day 7s intense fartlek session. It should feel no harsher than the hill session!

Phase Three: Anaerobic Threshold Running.

15K pace running is another fundamental ingredient to your endurance. 15K pace is easier to maintain than 10K pace, yet it's more beneficial because:

* It stimulates your anaerobic threshold to rise almost as much as 10K pace running does.
* While forcing you to run economically and concentrate on running form.
* Yet leaves your legs rested for your other speed training.

The serious half marathon trainer who runs fast once a week will replace the hills or fartlek with one quality threshold pace session per week for 6 weeks. Or, they could alternate a hilly fartlek session with threshold pace each week for 8 to 10 weeks.

Our moderately intense hero who runs fast twice a week will alternate fartlek with hills on Day Three, and run threshold pace on Day Seven.

Our highest intensity heroines will run one session every week of fartlek, hills and threshold pace.

All of you will continue to run long each weekend.

Injury prevention guidelines allow 10 percent of your mileage to be 15K pace, or five miles. Two times 2.5 miles; 5 x one mile; and a continuous 4 mile run, followed by a mile repeat at the same pace, gives a nice three week rotation. Start at 80 percent of maximum heartrate and increase pace to 85 or 90 percent. Begin these sessions at half-marathon pace and cruise up to 10 to 15 seconds per mile slower than your best recent 10K pace.

Shortage of local races at 10K or 10 miles? You can double your anaerobic session once a month instead of racing. Ten times one mile at 10 mile pace with a one minute rest, or five times two miles with a two minute rest are much easier sessions than a 10 mile race...provided you rest up for them with a low mileage week. However, most areas have a race at 10K to the half-marathon every 3 to 8 weeks. Slot these into your program and rest up for them.

Going longer than 6 weeks without a race of more than 5K? Do the big threshold pace session instead of a race. It's only 20 percent of your weekly mileage: your up-coming half marathon is 26 percent of your average weeks mileage! Most runners should run a 5K race once a month for:

* The joy of it...cruising at high speed with no expectation of personal records because you did not rest up.
* Socialization with numerous runners.
* A pleasant break from hill or threshold pace sessions.

Moderately intense runners.

Day 1: Long and gentle run. Continue to include an 18 each month. Increase pace toward 70 percent of maximum HR for the second half of each run.
Day 2: 5-mile run, plus 40 minutes of cross training.
Day 3: 8 miles: Alternate:

* A: 2.5 miles of hill repeats. Alternate long repeats and short hills.
* B: 5 miles of intense but relaxed fartlek.

Day 4: 60 minutes of gentle cross training.
Day 5: 10 miles steady, and ease back to 75 percent of maximum heartrate for your fast section because on...
Day 7: Do 7-9 miles with 5 miles at threshold pace.

Phase Four: VO2 Maximum Training.

Two-mile race pace to 5K pace training adds power to your muscle fibers, makes you a more economical runner and improves the amount of oxygen you can process...and therefore your speed potential.

Serious half marathon trainers will replace the threshold pace running, which had been a hill session, which had been a fartlek session, with the VO2 enhancing Intervals.

The moderately hard trainer can rotate hills, hilly fartlek and threshold running on Day Three, while running a series of VO2 max Intervals on Day Seven for 6 to 12 weeks.

The highest intensity 50 mile per week person can also do the VO2 sessions on Day Seven, but will run two quality sessions back to back on Days 3 and 5 such as:
Week One: Hills followed by threshold.
Week Two: Threshold followed by fartlek.
Week Three: Fartlek followed by hills.

The fourth week should only have one midweek quality run of hilly fartlek which includes a few long reps at threshold pace...so that you rest up for a long race at the weekend. Don't rest up for 5K races. Use 5K races as a substitute for your interval sessions once a month, and for the reasons outlined on the previous page.

The VO2 Intervals will progress from four to five miles as described in Chapter Eight. Keep doing your 8,000 meters of intervals at 5K pace until you have no serious muscle aches afterwards. You'll probably need to run each full session three times for your muscle fibers to fully adapt, and to teach yourself to relax and run economically. You can then consider increasing pace toward 2-mile speed for some of your repeats.

The long runs are unchanged during Phase Four.

Phase Five: Half-Marathon Peaking.

Rest and longer repeats at 2 mile to 10K race pace combine to give extra pep to your legs while maximizing your VO2 capacity.

The serious trainer replaces the short Intervals with half miles and 1,200 meter repeats at 5K pace. Three sessions of each should suffice. The last session 4 days pre-race could be 10 x 300 meters...a very modest session.

The moderately intense runner will reduce his or her midweek session of hills, or threshold, or fartlek to 3 to 4 miles of speed running in order to be fresh for the Day 7s long repeats, which can be the day before your long run!

Highest intensity runners can run three miles of short Intervals at 5K pace for relaxation midweek, followed by a shorter session of hills or threshold running two days later. These highly experienced runners may run mile repeats at 5K race pace on two of the six weekends leading into their race, though they may be content with the 800s and 1,200s. They'll probably run some 2Ks at 10K race pace too.

All of you can reduce the two midweek runs by one mile for the first two weeks, by two miles for the next two weeks, and by three for the penultimate two weeks. This takes your mileage down to the low 40s.

The next to last ingredient is your long run. Over the last six weeks, try 14, 16, 18, 16, 13 then a 10 the weekend before the race. You will have run close to a dozen 18s and it is four weeks pre-race, so you have plenty of time to recover. Your body also has plenty of time to make its physiological adaptations inspired by that run!

Note: Don't run the final few long runs any faster than your usual long run pace: you're supposed to be resting up! The last week will include those 300s, and a five mile run to give you 26 miles for the week. You'll be nicely rested for the half marathon.

Training table abbreviations:

E = Easy runs...at 60-70 percent of maximum heartrate.
F = Fartlek
H = Hill repeats
HF = Hilly fartlek...less vigorous than the hill session.
A = Anaerobic threshold pace running...15K speed.
V = VO2 maximum pace intervals...2 mile to 10K speed.
All types of quality running require a warm-up and cooldown of two to three miles each side of the speed running. As you will be doing five miles at speed (or 2.5 miles for hill training), most speed days are 9 to 11 miles.

<u>Serious Runners</u> usually move their legs fast once a week, but should also run two times one mile at close to half marathon pace during each long run. You're probably experienced with 40 miles per week training, but not yet ready for two full sessions of speed running per week at 50 miles. This author suggests:

* You do 2 to 3 miles of hilly fartlek at 15K to 5K intensities most Saturdays before your Sunday long run.
* Doing your main speed running midweek, but,
* Do only two to three weeks of each type of training because you'll lose the benefits of hill repeats if you wait too long before you race.
* Do the long repeats at 5K pace for the last two weeks.
* Run 5 miles on one of your easy days, say Tuesday, when you'll also run 12 to 16 x 100 meter striders.
* Cross train twice a week.

	Day One	Three	Four	Five	Seven
Probably...	*Sunday*	*Tues*	*Wed*	*Thurs*	*Saturday*
Week 1	15	5E	5F	8E	3HF
Week 2	18	5E	5F	8E	3HF
Week 3	15	5E	2.5H	8E	3F
Week 4	18	5E	2.5H	8E	3F
Week 5	15	5E	5A	10E	3F
Week 6	18	5E	5A	10E	3F
Week 7	12	5E	3HF	6E	Race 10K
Week 8	12	5E	4F	8E	3A
Week 9	18	5E	5A	10E	3HF
Week 10	17	5E	5A	10E	3F
Week 11	16	5E	5V	10E	3HF
Week 12	15	5E	5V	8E	3F
Week 13	14	5E	5V	10E	2.5HF
Week 14	13	4E	4V	8E	2F
Week 15	10	3E	2A	4E	Race your half marathon.

Moderate Intensity Runners do two full speed sessions a week, and can run 2 x one mile at close to half marathon pace during long runs. Spend the final 6 weeks running long repeats at 5K to 10K pace. Keep speed running relaxed at all times. Stretch and weight train to maintain balance. If the fartlek section is recovery from your previous long race, do 13s for your long runs. Gently transition into your next half marathon's training.

Strength is vital for distance running success. Cutting the hills is short sighted. Run plenty of hills and weight train during your VO2 max phases to maintain muscle strength.

Run 16 x 100 during your easy 5 miles each Monday.

Day	One	Three	Five	Seven
Probably...	*Sunday*	*Tues*	*Thurs*	*Saturday*
Weeks 1, 3,	15	5F	8E	5F
Weeks 2, 4,	18	4F	8E	4HF
Weeks 5, 7...13	15	5F	10E	2.5H
Weeks 6, 8...14	18	5HF	10E	2.5H
Week 15	12	3HF	6E	Race 10K
Week 16	15	4F	8E	4A
Wks 17, 19, 21	15	2.5H	10E	5A
Wks 18, 20, 22	18	5HF	10E	5A
Week 23	12	3HF	6E	Race 10 miles
Week 24	5E	3HF	8E	4V
Weeks 25 & 28	18	2.5H	10E	5V
Weeks 26 & 29	15	5A	10E	Race 5K
Weeks 27 & 30	18	5HF	10E	5V
Week 31	10	3A	5E	Race 10K
Week 32	15	4HF	8E	4V
Week 33	18	2.5H	10E	5V
Week 34	15	5A	10E	Race 5K
Week 35	18	3HF	10E	5V
Week 36	16	2H	9E	4V
Week 37	14	4A	8E	3V
Week 38	10	2V	2A	Race the half.

<u>Highest Intensity Runners</u> shift their legs rapidly during nearly every run. Two miles at close to half marathon pace practice is still useful during long runs. Run an easy five miles on your most convenient day, and like other 50 per weekers, cross train twice a week; your other days are:

	Day One	Three	Four	Five	Seven
Probably...	*Sunday*	*Tues*	*Wed*	*Thurs*	*Saturday*
Weeks 1 & 2	16	5F	5E	5HF	5F
Wks 3, 5,7, 9	15	5F	5E	5HF	2.5H
Wks 4, 6, 8, 10	18	5F	5E	5HF	2.5H
Week 11	13	3HF	5E	2F	Race 10K
Week 12	15	3F	5E	2H	4A
Wks 13, 15, 17	18	2.5H	5E	5HF	5A
Wks 14, 16, 18	15	5HF	5E	2.5H	5A
Week 19	12	3HF	4E	2F	Race 10K
Week 20	12	3F	5E	2H	4V
Weeks 21 & 24	18	5HF	5E	2.5H	5V
Weeks 22 & 25	16	2.5H	5E	5A	5V
Weeks 23 & 26	14	5HF	5E	5A	4V
Week 27	12	3A	3E	2F	Long Race
Week 28	5E	2F	5E	3HF	4V
Week 29	18	2H	5E	5V	4V
Week 30	20	5A	5E	2H	5V
Week 31	16	2H	5E	5A	10K race
Week 32	18	3HF	5E	5A	5V
Week 33	15	5V	5E	2H	4V
Week 34	13	3HF	3E	3A	3V
Week 35	10	2V	Rest	2A	4E

Race your half marathon, 30K or 20 miles.

Note that weeks 29 and 33 contain two sessions working on VO2 maximum. The midweek session is usually short repeats at 5K pace with the last mile of repeats at close to two mile pace. The weekend session is long repeats at 5K to 10K pace.

And at 60 miles per week.

The 18-mile run is a mere 30 percent of your weekly mileage, but you still need to control your speed. You now have sufficient miles to run that long mid-week run...with half of it at 15 seconds per mile slower than half marathon pace.

Most of you will do more than one speed session. A weekly three mile session of hilly fartlek gives a great transition between the different intensities, especially as you have six miles to play with in your main speed sessions.

Potential sessions include:

* 20 times a 300 meter hill;
* 10 times a half mile hill;
* 2 x 3 miles at half-marathon pace;
* 3 x 2 miles at 15K pace;
* 6 x one mile at 10K pace;
* 8 x 800 at 5K pace, followed by 8 x 400;
* 10 x 600 at 5K pace followed by 300s at 2 mile pace.
* Hour long fartlek sessions when you wander and change pace for 200 to 1,000 meters, or 40 seconds to 4 minutes depending on which system of counting you prefer.

Running 60 miles per week also allows you to:

* Run more 18s;
* Run a 20 once every 6 weeks if the mood strikes you;
* Include midweek fairly long runs of 12 to 13 miles;
* Include more speed running in quality sessions.

Five or six runs a week? Your choice, but here's the basic plan.

<u>Saturday:</u> Speed running or a race.
<u>Sunday:</u> Long recovery run.

Monday: Easy run and cross-train.
Tuesday: Maintain fast running skills from prior phases. Example: You are currently in your VO2 max phase and do 5K pace Intervals on Saturday. On Tuesdays during these 6-12 weeks, you'll alternate anaerobic threshold with hills.
Wednesday: Easy run and cross train.
Thursday: Up to 12 miles, with increasing amounts at close to half marathon pace. Examples: Week 22 would include 8 miles at 30 seconds slower than race pace; week 36 includes 5 miles at decent pace. You'll need to finish with an easy mile each Thursday. Friday is usually a full rest day.

	Sunday	M	Tu	W	Th	Sat
	Day One	*Two*	*Three*	*Four*	*Five*	*Seven*
Weeks 1, 3,	15	7E	5F	7E	10E	5F
Weeks 2, 4,	18	7E	6F	7E	10E	6HF
Weeks 5, 7...13	15	7E	6F	7E	12E	3H
Weeks 6, 8...14	18	7E	5HF	7E	12E	3H
Week 15	12	5E	4HF	6E	2F	Race
Week 16	12	7E	5F	7E	8E	5A
Wks 17, 19, 21	15	7E	3H	7E	12E	6A
Wks 18, 20, 22	18	7E	6HF	7E	12E	6A
Week 23	12	5E	4HF	6E	2F	Race
Week 24	12	7E	5HF	7E	8E	5V
Weeks 25 & 28	18	7E	3H	7E	12E	6V
Weeks 26 & 29	15	7E	6A	7E	12E	6V
Weeks 27 & 30	18	7E	6HF	7E	12E	6V
Week 31	10	5E	4A	5E	2F	Race
Week 32	12	7E	4HF	7E	8E	5V
Week 33	18	7E	2.5H	7E	12E	6V
Week 34	15	6E	6A	6E	11E	6V
Week 35	18	6E	4HF	6E	10E	5V
Week 36	16	5E	2H	5E	9E	4V
Week 37	14	4E	4A	4E	8E	3V
Week 38	10	Rest	2V	zero	2A	Race

your half marathon or 20 miles.

Some weekends it's nice to bring Saturday's session forward and train hard on the Friday. However, those of you who prefer the medium run to be on Thursdays may be too fatigued for a quality speed session on Friday, so you'll probably rest on Friday for a speedy Saturday on fresh legs.

Peaking for your race requires a combination of reduced mileage and a reduction of your other training to allow your muscles to adapt from prior weeks training.

Prudent use of long repeats when resting.

Used to 3 x 2 miles at 15K pace? Try two times 2.5 miles.

Used to 6 times 1,200 meters at 5K pace...try 3 times 2,000 meters at 5K pace.

Like 10 x 600 meters at 2 mile pace...try 6 x 800 at 2 mile pace.

Those three original sessions were 6, 4.5 and 3.75 miles, for a total of 14.25 at speed. The new sessions are 5, 3.75 and 3 miles, for a total of 11.75 miles, and give you a higher percentage of time in your training heartrate zone.

During the last two weeks you can cut an additional mile off of each speed session to give yourself about nine miles of quality running over the last 10 to 14 days pre-race. Example:

* 4 miles tempo. Two at half marathon pace, then two at 15K pace.
* 2K at 10K pace; 3 x 400 meters at 5K pace; one mile at 10K pace.
* 4 x 800 meters at 2 mile pace.

Your final speed session will usually be 8 to 10 times 300 meters at modest tempo, about 5K pace, with relaxed form.

Runners doing more than 60 miles per week

can easily adapt these schedules to meet their needs. Few people do more than 6 miles of quality in one session. Most of you will simply add a few easy runs at 70 percent of your maximum HR, and hopefully a few pickups to relax between your current quality sessions and long runs. Good luck to you all.

According to brilliant researcher David Costill, Ph.D. of Ball State University, adding more mileage does little to improve your VO2 max. Rather than risk injury with more miles, once you've reached 60 to 80 miles of steady running increase the quality of your mileage.

Change a quarter mile each month to anaerobic threshold, or hill running, or interval training or as striders to practice good running form. Make your mileage count.

Make your stretching count too. You can stretch almost anywhere during a five minute break while waiting to do something. See the back cover for the calf and of course the Achilles tendon stretch. Keep the heels on the ground.

Taken from Appendix Four

Don't let the doctors worry you.

Long runs result in minor muscle breakdown, which gives off chemical signs similar to the muscle damage of a heart attack. It is not usually your heart muscle which is damaged. It's simply the wear and tear from a pleasant yet long run. Eat some nice meals with normal protein amounts and your muscles will be stronger within a few days. Stay well hydrated to prevent blood clots though.

Runners do have heart attacks. When the ER doctor checks your creatine kinase-MB or other indicator of muscle damage, remind him or her about your most recent harsh training. Your EKG is also likely to suggest heart trouble due to PVCs and slow rate. A competent specialist will spot the athletic nature of your rhythm...especially if you let her know you're an athlete.

Chapter Fifteen

Post Race Fatigue Prevention

and some more

Running Rules & Tips

The most important exercise session is the one following your half-marathon. Take note of the recovery tips in Chapter Four for just after you've done a quality training session, and consider these additional tips.

Eight or 24 hours post race, walk a couple of miles and take another warm shower, then stretch. Session two could be another walk or an easy 3-mile run. Session three might be a one-hour bike ride if you were used to riding prior to the race. Then ease back up to steady 5 and 6 mile runs and gentle striders once your aches have diminished.

Want to run the half marathon four minutes faster? Lose 10 pounds in 26 weeks while weight training. Each pound of fat slows you by one to two seconds per mile, so 10 pounds should shave 2:10 to 4:20 off your half marathon.

<u>Doing any session for the first time?</u> Don't do much. First run in 5 years? Walk for 5 minutes to warm up, start your run very slowly and ease to a walk after one hundred yards or meters. Walk / run a mile. Shower and stretch gently.

<u>First speed session?</u> Run half a mile of repeats at the appropriate pace. Run 30 seconds slower than 5K pace to

improve your endurance and anaerobic threshold, and run a separate session at 5K pace to improve your running economy and oxygen uptake or VO2 maximum. Do not run at mile pace unless you are going to race the mile.

Hills build speed and character...provided you choose the right grade for your fitness level. Run small hills gently to start, increase intensity over several weeks, and then move up to short steep sections after a few months. Run at 5K intensity mostly, but find a long gentle hill and run up at lower intensity some weeks.

Start every session gently. Aiming for 5 miles in 50 minutes, which you know will be 75 percent of your maximum heartrate? Run the first mile in 10.5 minutes, pick up your pace ending the fourth mile at 9:45 pace before easing back to 10 minute pace to finish. Better yet, walk 200 meters before and after the run.

Speed sessions too. Run the first two repeats or the first half a mile a bit slower than goal pace for the session. Example: Want 8 x 400 meters in 90 seconds because you race the 5K in 19 minutes. Run two repeats each at 92, 90 and 88 before showing your self control with 89s to finish.

If you want a change of pace come race day, you'll need to practice it in training. Looking for six-minute miles and a surge? Run 800 meters with the first lap in 92 seconds and the second lap in 88 seconds. The "differential" is 16 seconds per mile. Think "running form" for the second lap.

Take long rests in speed training at first. Those 800s may need a four-minute rest the first time. Edge the recovery down by 30 seconds per month until you reach 60 seconds.

Treadmills get you off of the treadmill of life. You can do most types of speed running on the treadmill. You don't have to run downhill, so treadmills are especially good for hill training. Water is close by, there may be a TV on the wall, and you can get out of the heat or the cold. You avoid street dangers from dogs and people. Impact is softer than asphalt, reducing injury risk.

Provided the treadmill is set up properly, you can run precise workouts. This author tested three treadmills at his health club recently using a heartrate monitor set at threshold pace. The treadmills ranged from 6:22 to 6:00 per mile at a HR of 162. In April 2,002, a major manufacturer recalled nearly 6,000 young treadmills, which had a tendency to speed up. That said, it's still nice to work on running form indoors once a week for a treat.

Motivate yourself with a race once a month. Races give you an added reason to rest for a week and make your game more sociable. Rest usually means doing 60 percent of your average weekly mileage. Races give you an incentive to run 5 times 800 meters at 10 seconds per mile faster than your last 5K race, because it sets you up for your next race.

Feeling unmotivated for days at a time? Dissatisfied with your running and performances? Heartrate elevated when you wake up? You could have been overtraining. Decrease mileage for a few days or several weeks if necessary.

To avoid overtraining, set realistic goals which you can achieve based on current fitness, not based on your dream fitness level. Run a few striders of 200 meters at 5K pace twice a week for the joy of it rather than to train for a race. Slow down to 65 percent of maximum heartrate for most running. Cross train gently for recreation and a social life.

Drafting is legal, saves your energy, and can be worth a minute during a half marathon. The other runners must be at your desired pace, so don't run too fast in order to stay with a group. Pace dropping? It's your turn to set the pace, so expect others to draft behind you. Don't weave to drop them; in a mile, you could be drafting off them again!

<u>Don't race your friends.</u> You may be able to run 15 miles with him every Sunday, but his 5K speed can be 30 seconds per mile faster than yours. Race the first mile with him and you're destined to pain and slowing in the remainder of the race. Start at realistic pace for you.

Don't race your friend in training either. While it's nice to be more compatible, you can train with someone about 2 minutes faster than you are at the 5K. While she runs long repeats at anaerobic threshold, you can run short ones at 5K pace by doing the first and last lap of her mile repeat.

Smaller 5K disparity? Have the faster runners start 2 to 4 seconds after you do. Or perhaps you are the one who gets to start a few seconds later so that you can chase down your friends. If every runner goes at his or her appropriate speed, you should all reach the finish of the repeat at the same moment, though with different times for the distance.

<u>Tie your training and racing shoes with a double knot.</u> Lightweight training or performance shoes are best for long races: they give you more protection than racing flats.

<u>Weight train and cross train</u> until the last week before a big race. Don't increase the number of repeats, of sets, or the weight lifted in the last month. Instead, decrease repeats from 12 to 10 and then to 8 over the last three weeks to rest up. Weight train at 4 or 5 day intervals instead of every 3 days. Put your muscles through a full range of motion the last week while lifting only 75 percent of your usual weight...about seven days pre-race.

<u>Wear lightweight sweats to stay warm</u> during and after your warmup. Stretch gently before races and speed running.

Then wear the smallest amount of clothing conducive to the law and the conditions.

You cannot convert fat to muscle. They are two distinct body tissues. Exercise regularly and with modest increases in duration or resistance and you'll build larger and stronger muscle fibers. Occasionally you may even notice actual muscle size changes. If you exercise more than you used too while consuming the same number of calories, you'll lose weight...generally via fat cells decreasing in size.

You cannot body sculpt. Sadly, you cannot decide which part of your body fat leaves from. Sit-ups will not affect your stomach bulge, except to the extent that your posture may improve. The leg press will not improve the shape of your buns until you've burned off sufficient fat for those underlying muscles to show through a thinner fat layer.

Eat tones of complex carbohydrates. It is not excessive carbohydrate which makes you gain weight: Excess total calories per year is the culprit. Complex diabetics need to consume complex sugar. Complex athletes also need to consume complex sugar. Just like diabetics, keep your intake of simple sugars low.

You burn more "net" fat with fast running. Fast running is less efficient, so you burn a few more calories per mile.

Fast running allows you to run farther in your 40 minutes, so you burn more calories. The "net calorie burn" dictates how much fat you'll lose from your body. The fuel you actually burn while running fast will be sugar at certain speeds; after the run, your body will convert its fat store to replace the sugar which you burned off. You also burn more calories after quality exercise because your metabolic system remains at high intensity for longer.

You don't need protein supplements. Keep protein consumption modest because it's exercise which builds larger muscle fibers: muscle development uses minimal amounts of protein per day.

The most important nutrient is water. Focus on the water, not what form it comes in. Most sports drinks contain too much sugar. Water is absorbed just as fast, and unless you're training for over two hours, water is all you need.

You sweat out very little salt. Pleasant tasting food will give you all the replacement you need...provided you include some fruit and vegetables.

Breakthroughs in life usually come from moderate amounts of effort on a consistent basis. You study all year toward your high grades: cramming can get you a few extra points, but most people are locked into a grade by the final few days. Overnight success takes years of preparation!

Even more so with running. Cram in extra runs or more speedwork in the days pre-race and you'll bomb in the race due to excessive fatigue. A series of runs over many months, plus rest, sets you up for improved fitness and faster races. See also Yakovlev's model starting on page 46.

Don't ever "hammer" your workout. Instead, enjoy your exercise. It annoys me to read experts who say you need to get sufficient rest on your easy days so that you can hammer your hard workouts. Work is something you do for 8 to 12 hours a day, but you don't go all out in the first minute...unless your goal is to be asleep with exhaustion after half an hour.

True, your easy running days should be less intense than your hard training days. However, you should never be hammering your harsher exercise days.

* You run long efforts at 15K pace to improve your anaerobic threshold;
* You run at 5K to 2 mile pace for one to two minute repeats to improve your VO2 maximum and your running efficiency;
* You run some uphills for extra strength...but again, only at 5K intensity.

The last couple of repeats will usually feel harder than the first few, but you should not feel hammered because you will spend months building up to these longer sessions.

Mix in rest days and long runs every 7 days, and your two quality sessions each week will not give you sore muscles which take days to recover from. They will gradually prepare you for higher levels of health and fitness, or great races.

<u>Still looking for an illusive personal record?</u> Get a friend to pace you accurately for several key tempo and VO2 max sessions, and to pace you on a gently downhill half marathon course such as Las Vegas, at a temperature of about 50 degrees Fahrenheit, after resting up properly: a PR is highly probable.

<u>Your physiological racing limits</u> are based partly on your natural abilities and on how much and how sensible your training is. If adding more training (usually mileage) does not make you slower (overtraining), or injure you (overtraining), or bore you, you can add training each year or until you beat arbitrary barriers such as 90 minutes.

Want to take your half-marathon running to the next level? Go back and spend another year concentrating on the 10K with *10K & 5K Running, Training & Racing*. Improve your 10K by one minute, then come back to take 2 minutes and 13 seconds off your half-marathon.

Appendix I

Anaerobic threshold is 10K pace if your 10K PR is slower than 45 minutes, 15K pace for most runners, but Half-marathon pace for top runners. Times in this table are for mile repeats. Use 85 percent of MHR to guide your upper training pace limit.

The 15K PR line is your projected PR based on your 10K time...provided you're running sufficient mileage, and doing hills and intervals at 5K pace. Do some threshold training with longer repeats such as 2 miles and with 4-mile tempo runs.

Note: one way to move up the table, to improve PRs, is to train for that upper line. Currently doing 6.51 mile repeats with a 90 second rest because your 10K PR is 41.15, and because 15K pace improves your anaerobic threshold while leaving your muscles fresh? At some stage, you'll increase speed toward 6.39 miles and feel relaxed doing it, and your heartrate will remain below 90 percent of max. 6.40 is 15K pace for your next level!

Once you can run 4 or 5 repeats at 6.39 without a rest week leading into the session, you may be ready for some PRs. Moving up a line can take months. Try 5 seconds per mile steps rather than jumping up a line. Don't kid yourself into thinking you're in PR shape by taking an easy week prior to mile repeats. Rest up for a 10K or 15K race to check your progress.

When increasing mileage, run your repeats at the slower end of your range. Run half-marathon pace if you're in the top two-thirds of the table; run 15K pace if in the lower third. Increase to 15K and 10K pace respectively once you've got used to your increased mileage. The anaerobic threshold Pace for Mile Repeats table is on page 203.

Anaerobic Threshold Pace for Mile Repeats:

PR at 5K	PR at 10K	10K pace	Best 15K	15K pace	Half-marathon pace	Half-marathon finish time
14:57	30:54	4:59	48:19	5:11	5:24	70:45
15:31	32:02	5:10	50:02	5:22	5:37	73:34
16:05	33:10	5:20	51:34	5:32	5:47	75:46
16:39	34:20	5:32	53:27	5:44	5:59	78:23
17:11	35:27	5:43	55:09	5:55	6:10	80:47
17:45	36:37	5:54	56:51	6:06	6:24	83:50
18:20	37:50	6:06	58:44	6:18	6:36	86:28
18:54	39:00	6:17	60:26	6:29	6:47	88:52
19:27	40:09	6:28	62:09	6:40	7:00	91:42
20:00	41:15	6:39	63:51	6:51	7:11	94:06
20:34	42:23	6:49	65:24	7:01	7:21	96:17
21:07	43:29	7:01	67:34	7:15	7:35	99:21
21:41	44:40	7:12	69:17	7:26	7:48	102:11
22:18	45:56	7:24	71:09	7:38	8:00	104:48
23:06	47:35	7:40	73:38	7:54	8:19	108:57
23:56	49:18	7:56	76:07	8:10	8:35	112:27
24:46	50:41	8:10	78:56	8:26	8:51	115:43
25:36	52:44	8:30	81:43	8:46	9:16	121:24
26:33	54:41	8:48	84:30	9:04	9:34	125:20
27:24	56:26	9:05	86:50	9:19	9:54	129:41
29:10	60:06	9:41	93:12	10:00	10:40	139:44
30:25	62:42	10:08	97:33	10:28	11:08	145:51
33:36	69:16	11:09	107:12	11:30	12:15	160:29

The half marathon finish times (last column) are based on the pace of the mile repeats which precede them. A 91:42 half runner should do repeats at 7 minutes per mile or a bit quicker to improve her anaerobic threshold. Table adapted from page 274 of *Running Dialogue*, by David Holt.

Appendix II

The VO2 Max Pace Chart on the next page is based on 2 mile, 5K and 10K paces, which means running at 100, 95 and 90 percent of VO2 max, or at about 98, 95 and 92 percent of maximum heartrate.

If the 400s feel easy, but you have difficulty maintaining pace on the 800s or 1,200s, you may lack background base endurance. Runs at 70 percent of max HR build base aerobic ability.

If the 400s feel harsh, incorporate 100s etc., to work on form at speed. Then run some 200s and 300s before trying the 400s again. Relaxed running at 2 mile pace takes practice. Don't let 400s dominate; you can run 600s at 2 mile pace also.

You have to set the limit on the number of reps. You can ignore the 10 percent mileage rule once a month. Rest up to peak with a five-mile training session. Or, ease through more reps at 10 to 12 seconds per mile slower (10K pace).

Try quarters at three seconds per repeat slower than usual so as to hit 10K pace, which is 90 percent of VO2 max: half of the reps should still be close to 5K pace. Run the second half of your intervals faster, or alternate a 5K pace rep with a 10K pace rep. When you've done a particular session three or four times over 12 weeks, ease more reps toward 5K pace.

Try really long repeats at 10K pace. See page 157.

Remember: your reps should be about 3 seconds per lap faster than 10K pace to represent 5,000 pace; 5 seconds a lap faster than 10K pace to equal your two mile potential.

Got a good eye? You may notice that mile repeats at 10K pace are in this VO2 max and the anaerobic training chart.

Interval paces at 100 to 90 percent of VO2 max.

PR at 2 mile	400s @ 2M pace	800s @5K pace	PR at 5K	1,200s @5K pace	PR @ 10K	mile reps at 10K pace
9:19	69.8	2:23.6	14:57	3:35	30:54	4:59
9:40	72.5	2:29	15:31	3:44	32:02	5:10
10:02	75.2	2:34.4	16:05	3:52	33:10	5:20
10:23	77.9	2:39.8	16:39	4:00	34:20	5:32
10:44	80.5	2:45	17:11	4:08	35:27	5:43
11:06	83.2	2:50.4	17:45	4:16	36:37	5:54
11:28	86	2:56	18:20	4:24	37:50	6:06
11:50	88.7	3:01.4	18:54	4:32	39:00	6:17
12:11	1:31.4	3:06.8	19:27	4:40	40:09	6:28
12:32	1:34	3:12	20:00	4:48	41:15	6:39
12:54	1:36.7	3:17.4	20:34	4:56	42:23	6:49
13:15	1:39.4	3:22.8	21:07	5:04	43:29	7:01
13:37	1:42.1	3:28.2	21:41	5:12	44:40	7:12
14:00	1:45	3:34	22:18	5:20	45:56	7:24
14:31	1:48.9	3:41.8	23:06	5:33	47:35	7:40
15:03	1:52.9	3:49.8	23:56	5:45	49:18	7:56
15:35	1:56.9	3:57.8	24:46	5:57	50:41	8:10
16:07	2:01	4:05.8	25:36	6:09	52:44	8:30
16:40	2:05	4:15	26:33	6:22	54:41	8:48
17:12	2:09	4:23	27:24	6:34	56:26	9:05
18:16	2:17	4:39	29:10	7:00	60:06	9:41
19:01	2:22.6	4:54	30:25	7:21	62:42	10:08
21:30	2:41	5:23	33:36	8:03	69:16	11:09

Long repeats, or short repeats with short rests keep you at your training heartrate for a greater percentage of your training time. Both feel harder than short Intervals with long rests. Once you're used to 4 or 5 miles of short reps, *gradually* change over to short rests. As you get fitter, your long reps will need short rests too.

Appendix III

Low Mileage Half-Marathon.

Chapter Twelve's 40 miles per week program also shows you a three days per week running schedule that lets you prepare for a half marathon on 30 miles per week. Pages 171-172 show your key sessions, which are:

* 3 miles of speed running within an 8 mile run;
* One day with 12-16 striders within your 8 miles; and,
* The long run averaging 14 miles, but with two miles at close to half marathon pace.

Cross-train on two days, and 30 miles of running will still get you a half marathon quite safely.

In fact, take walking breaks and anyone can complete a half-marathon. While it's better to have several years running background at the 5K and 10K before you attempt a half-marathon, most people can complete 13.1 miles.

It only takes 20 to 25 miles a week to run-walk a half-marathon. It won't be fast; but it doesn't have to be ugly; you can run-walk a "half" with only modest injury risk.

You do most of what 50 mile a week runners do, but do it every two weeks. Run short efforts <u>and</u> tempo pace every week to maintain good running form and leg speed. There's also a long run at close to half marathon pace.

Multiply your 10K race time by 2.4 (higher mileage people can use 2.2 to 2.3, but you will be taking walk breaks), and divide by 13.1 to get your running pace. A 50-minute 10K runner (eight minute miles) gets 120 minutes, or about nine minutes and 10 seconds per minute mile. Starting at 40 minutes on Day One of week one, add five minutes, or half a mile on every odd numbered week until you get to 10 miles or 100 minutes of continuous running at 15 seconds per mile slower than goal pace.

* Odd numbered weeks
Day one...15 seconds per mile slower than half marathon pace. 12 increases over 24 weeks gets you to 100 minutes.
Days two & five...walk a mile, run two, and walk a mile. In the early weeks, this can remain a thirty-minute run.
Day three and seven...rest
Day four...Alternate long reps and a tempo run at anaerobic threshold. Keep doing 2 to 3 miles of fairly fast running.
Day six...fartlek, or 100s, or 200s. Keep good form and improve your oxygen uptake system.
These 20-25 miles set you up for day one of Even weeks.

* Even weeks.
Day one...Run-walk starting with 60 minutes. Add ten minutes each time to give you three hours (but no more than 14 miles) at 24 weeks. Keep the running at one minute per mile slower than half marathon target pace. Run 15 minutes, and then walk at relaxed tempo for five. Practice taking in liquids with a little carbohydrate. You can also run 10 minutes and walk one minute if it suits you better.
Days two-four...restive, but do 20 to 30 minutes of exercise on two days, including a two mile run.
Day five....A--Once a month do hill repeats, but slowly. They are described in Chapter Three. If you prefer, do reps through mud. But do do this strength session. Hill training is very important for half marathon running: You need all the anatomical benefits which resistance training will give you. Six to eight long hill reps are better than short ones.

B--On the even number weeks when you don't do hills, run intervals on the track. Sorry, did I say this was a minimalist schedule! Read Chapter Eight.
Try these six sessions:

* 6 x 400; 5 x 600; 8 x 400; 4 x 800; 8 x 400; 6 x 600;
* Run them at 5K pace or 10 to 15 seconds per mile faster (VO2 max pace). Take the same distance as rest and jog it. Clearly a vital day's training; you've had three rest days...so make the most of it, but don't run faster than two mile pace.
Day six...walk one, run two, and walk one
Day seven...rest

* Resting up: The last walk-run prior to your race should be an hour less than your longest. Two times one mile at race pace is the only speed session in the last week.

Gear everything toward the long runs to build aerobic base. Speed sessions give the benefits of every type of training which international class runner's use.

You'll be able to run-walk the half marathon after six months. Hopefully, you'll do a few 10Ks in the build-up. You can also stay at week 25s level for some time. The longer you remain at week 24-25's level, by repeating it several times; the more you do on your easy days--the more likely you will be able to run most of the race at half marathon target pace with minimal walks. Resting up may allow you to run for 30 minutes at a time with a five-minute walk break, or 15 minutes with a one-minute walk break. If you sense you're approaching poop-doom, settle back to 20 or 15 running alternating with five minutes walk.

Training table abbreviations:

40@M = number of minutes at or 15 seconds per mile slower than half marathon pace.
CI2 = 2 miles of Cruise Intervals (anaerobic threshold);
H2 = Two miles of hill training.
T2 = Tempo 2 miles.
70 WR = alternate walking with running at 60 seconds per mile slower than half marathon pace.
6 x 400 = no faster than 5K pace.

2F, 20 x 100 or 16 x 200 = Run these striders on soft surfaces at no faster than 5K pace.
Also…cross train twice a week. Include strength and aerobic training…from Chapters 9 and 10.

Low mileage recreational Half-marathon.

	Day One	Two	Four	Five	Six
Week 1	40@M	4WR	CI2	4WR	2F
Two	60WR	Run 20 minutes		20 mins	H2
Three	45@M	4WR	T2	4WR	20 x 100
Four	70WR	20 mins		20 mins	6 x 400
Five	50@M	4WR	CI2	4WR	2F
Six	80WR	Run 30 minutes		30 mins	H2
Seven	55@M	4WR	T2	4WR	16 x 200
Eight	90WR	30 mins		30 mins	5 x 600
Nine	60@M	4WR	CI2.5	4WR	2F
Ten	100WR	30 mins		30 mins	H2
Eleven	65@M	4WR	T2.5	4WR	24 x 100
Twelve	110WR	30 mins		30 mins	8 x 400
Thirteen	70@M	4WR	CI3	4WR	2F
Fourteen	120WR	30 mins		30 mins	H2
Fifteen	75@M	4WR	T3	4WR	20 x 200
16	130WR	30 mins		30 mins	4 x 800
17	80@M	4WR	CI3	4WR	3F
18	140WR	30 mins		30 mins	H2
19	85@M	4WR	T3	4WR	30 x 100
20	150WR	30 mins		30 mins	8 x 400
21	90@M	4WR	CI3	4WR	3F
22	160WR	30 mins		30 mins	H2
23	95@M	4WR	T3	4WR	20 x 200
24	180WR	25 mins		25 mins	6 x 600
25	100@M	4WR	CI3	4WR	3F
26	120WR	20 mins		20 mins	6 x 400
27	50@M	3WR	CI2	Rest	2WR
28	Race				

Appendix IV

19 Side Effects

As promised on page 8, here's a summary of the health benefits of regular exercise...adapted from 5K Fitness Run, and "Why Exercise" at www.runningbook.com

Exchange running for walking if you like. Running gives the same health benefits when done at appropriate intensity.

Injections of Human Growth Hormone turn back your body clock by decades. Human Growth Hormone:

* Increases muscle mass,
* Strengthens bones,
* Increases stamina and vitality,
* Increases cardiac output and energy,
* Decreases blood pressure,
* Improves cholesterol profile,
* Improves sleep and vision,
* Improves psychological well-being and memory,
* Strengthens the immune system, and,
* Increases fertility, sexual desire and performance.

But you don't need injections to get Human Growth Hormone (HGH). Regular doses of exercise will stimulate your body to produce its own HGH. Exercise is much cheaper than hormonal injections and less painful. Run at the right intensity and there's no pain with exercise.

The secrets to gaining health benefits from exercise are:

* To exercise regularly;
* To exercise at a brisk pace for the middle section several times each week; and,
* To exercise for about forty minutes at a time. (But do a bit more occasionally.)

1. Walking extends your life.

Heart disease is the leading cause of death nationwide, killing more than 950,000 people in the U.S. each year.

According to a 12-year study, (New England Journal of Medicine, Jan 8, 1998), retired men who walked more than 2 miles a day lived longer than those who walked less than a mile a day. Only 23.8% of the 14 mile plus per week group died during that time; 40.5% died from the lower mileage group died during the study period.

Walking reduces heart attack risk and aids weight lose.

Women too! 3 hours per week of brisk walking decreased heart attacks by nearly 40 percent. 5 hours per week ladies cut their risk by over 50 percent. (According to an analysis of the 72,488 women in the Nurses Health Study).

Don't give yourself a heart attack in the first few weeks of exercise. Start gently and stay hydrated. At rest or during exercise, if you feel fullness, tightness, pressure or pain in the center of your chest; if the pain spreads to your shoulders, neck, back or arms; if you break into a cold sweat, feel lightheaded or short of breath, call 911.

Red wine (a glass a day) has been shown to improve circulation, but so has black tea. Four cups of tea give enough antioxidants or flavonoids to help the endothelium or inner lining of blood vessels. Healthy endothelium expands as the blood flow increases making you less likely to get heart disease. You still need to eat your veggies and fruit and you still need to exercise. Apples and apple juice contain tannins, which have anti-adhesion properties, also reducing the risk of circulatory diseases.

Omega-3 fats protect the heart and blood vessels from damage, so consume oily fish such as salmon, tuna and cod, or flaxseed (and its oil), pumpkin seeds and nuts. The prostaglandins made from omega-3s tell blood vessels to dilate, keep your blood fluid, and reduce inflammation, which is good for your muscles and your mind.

Have unusual chest pain which lasts for more than a few minutes? Get some medical attention. Heartburn, courtesy of the contents of your stomach, shows itself with a sharp burning sensation below the ribs especially soon after eating. Symptoms are eased with antacids. You probably will not be in a cold sweat.

Use these simple guidelines to decrease heartburn:

* Eat minimal protein in the 2 hours before exercise because it slows the emptying of your stomach.
* Eat minimal fat in the 2 hours before exercise because it stimulates the release of bile into your stomach.
* Keep fiber to a minimal for that last pre-run meal.
* Which leaves you your trusty carbohydrates. Monitor intake of citrus fruits, any drink with more than 6 percent sugar (dilute them with water), and caffeine.
* Spicy or fatty food can affect you for 6 hours or more.
* Stay hydrated before and during runs. Liquid sloshing around in your stomach for more than 15 minutes? There's probably too much sugar in it, so drink some water.

Control your quality run or race anxiety or your stomach emptying will be delayed. Can't control yourself with relaxation techniques? Allow an extra hour or two after your last snack before running.

2. Walking lowers Stroke risk.

Stroke or cerebrovascular accident (CVA) is the third biggest killer, taking about 160,000 American lives per year, but they're not accidents if you can prevent them.

Burning 2,000 calories cuts your stroke risk by nearly half according to one study (Stroke, Oct 1998).

Your exercise need only be moderately intensive. Brisk walking, dancing, bicycling or running fit the bill. Exercise at work also decreases stroke risk.

Exercise protects against stroke by modifying risk factors such as high blood pressure, body weight, and blood clots:

Exercise also improves your brains circulation due to less plaque being laid down in the vital arteries.

Stroke is also called a cerebral vascular accident or CVA, but if you can reduce your CVA risk by half with simple exercise, a CVA is not an accident: a CVA is the result of neglecting to exercise.

Poor circulation is the first and third leading cause of death. What is the second biggest murderer? Smoking and second hand smoke is the second leading cause of death in the US. Smokers are 20 times more likely to get lung cancer and even more likely to die from the cancer. Smokers are 40 percent more likely to get colorectal cancer. Due to cancers being more advanced and the people being unhealthy, smokers are more likely to die soon after diagnosis too. Avoid smokers to extend your life and exercise regularly to enjoy your life.

3. Save your gallbladder.

According to a study at the Harvard School of Public Health, women who exercise two to three hours per week cut their gallbladder surgery by 31 percent compared with women who don't exercise at all.

More than 300,000 women have their gallbladders taken out each year. Obesity and rapid weight loss increase the risk of gallstones. Lose weight slowly and permanently!

This author has been nursing for 25 years, and has yet to see a slim person have gallbladder surgery.

As 80 percent of the gallstones in this country are solid cholesterol, lowering your cholesterol level should help to avoid the gallbladder cut.

Women with desk jobs are more likely to need their gallbladders removed...especially if you are also inactive in your recreational habits.

As with prostate and most other surgeries, regular exercise and being active decreases surgery complications.

4. Wake up! Exercise decreases blood pressure.

The higher your blood pressure is, the higher your risk of circulatory diseases. Use regular exercise and healthy eating to lower your risk from a slew of hypertension related ailments. Hypertension increases the hearts workload.

No time for exercise? According to researchers at McMaster University in Hamilton, Ontario, 10 minutes of aerobic exercise will decrease blood pressure. Twenty to 30 minutes would be better, but surely you can find 10 minutes to preserve your life. Morticians can't preserve your life; regular exercise will delay your visit to the mortician!

5. Exercise decreases the severity and the side effects from diabetes.

Exercise can control adult onset or Type 2 diabetes. Type 2 diabetes messes with the way your body utilizes sugar. In type 2 diabetes, either your body makes insufficient insulin, or your body can't use the insulin very well. With either scenario, your body can't move the sugar from your blood, into your cells. The sugar level in your bloodstream rises. Every exercise session you add reduces your diabetes risk.

Regular exercise stimulates and improves your cells ability to take in sugar, thus lowering your blood sugar level toward the normal range. Regular exercise such as walking or running will also help you to lose weight, decreasing the amount of insulin needed to keep your blood sugar in that normal range.

Who is affected by Type II Diabetes? Mostly the over 45s, overweight and inactive people. Type 2 diabetes runs in families too. Overweight, inactive families! Half the Americans who have diabetes may not know it!

Lose enough weight and do enough exercise and you can control type 2 diabetes. According to a Finnish study, losing 10 pounds reduced the incidence of type 2 diabetes by 58 percent in those who were at high risk for diabetes.

6. Stronger bones & fewer fractures from osteoporosis.

According to the Journal of Bone and Mineral Research, vol. 12, 1997, women over the age of 50 who currently walk (or cycle outdoors) for more than 30 minutes a day are 20 % less likely to develop dowager's hump as a result of osteoporosis. Menopause puts women at risk for losing calcium and increases heart disease risk. Exercise reduces these menopausal risks.

Achieve a one percent increase in bone mass and you decrease your fracture risk by 2 percent. Or simply hold on to that one percent in the first place with exercise. Men who run 9 times per month have 8 percent greater bone density compared to inactive guys!

Exercise involving gentle ground impact builds more bone than rhythmic exercise without ground impact. Running or walking is great for preventing osteoporosis. Running up-hills builds bone as do weight bearing squats in preference to the leg press.

You'll need to consume calcium too of course. The average person's consumption is 250 milligrams short of the RDA for calcium. Add an extra yogurt or glass of low fat milk or serving of broccoli and you will almost be up to 1,200 milligrams for the day.

7. Cholesterol.

According to a pilot study by Dr. Kraus at Duke University, exercising for one hour, four times per week for three months reduced LDL or bad cholesterol from 122 to 104 on average. HDL or good cholesterol rose from 32 to 37, making for stupendous improvements in their HDL to LDL ratio, moving from 3.81 to 2.81.

The American Heart Association regards low levels of "good" cholesterol to be a risk factor for heart disease. Low levels of high-density lipoprotein (HDL)...below 35 milligrams per deciliter...gives you greater heart attack risk.

More than one in five men with heart disease suffer from low HDL despite owning safe levels of low-density lipoprotein (LDL), or "bad" cholesterol.

All people, especially people with low HDL should do aerobic exercise on a regular basis to raise their HDL levels. The result will be a reduction in the death rate from heart disease. High mileage people have the best HDL levels, so even after your half marathon is done, run long once every two weeks, and maintain decent mileage.

8. Decrease belly fat and body weight.

Trim your belly and get rid of tummy fat. According to a ten-year study of 44,000 women, walking 4 or more hours per week reduced women's risk of gaining weight around their waists by 16 %. According to JAMA October 27, 1999, about 300,000 people per year die in the U.S. from obesity related diseases. Especially items 1 and 2 above.

The best way to lose belly fat is to exercise more and to eat less. Crunches and sit-ups will tone the muscles, but they burn very few calories. Any aerobic exercise for 40 minutes at modest intensity is the way to burn calories.

Healthy snacks made up of bulky carbohydrates like apples and bulky veggies such as broccoli, carrots and potatoes, also decrease the likelihood of you noshing on high calorie snacks like cookies. Although you'll want to include legumes such as peas for their protein and minerals, bulky vegetables are more filling and send the "I'm full signal" to your brain for fewer calories than legumes.

9. Decrease eyesight loss from Glaucoma.

Exercise improves your eyesight. Glaucoma is the leading cause of vision loss and blindness in the U.S.; it is the result of an increase in eye pressure. When sedentary people began a three times a week, brisk walking program, those with glaucoma reduced their eye pressure by 20 percent.

People without glaucoma also experienced a 9 percent reduction in eye pressure. (American Academy of Ophthalmology's annual meeting, Oct 1997).

10. Walking decreases the pain of arthritis.

Regular exercise stimulates thicker cartilage between your bones, and better muscle strength to keep your joints stable. Regular runners are five times less likely to have knee problems than sedentary folk.

11. Exercise elevates mood and the enjoyment of time spent on this planet.

Regular exercise is an effective way to release tension and reduce anxiety. Exercise uses up some of those debilitative fight or flight chemicals. Exercise reduces stress levels, releases muscle tension and has fewer side effects than sedatives!

Beat depression: According to research at Duke University, 30 minutes of moderate running on three days a week is as effective as medication for the clinically depressed. Exercisers also improved their concentration, planning and organization. There are unpleasant side effects from Prozac and other pills. The main side effect from exercise is a stronger heart to cope with life's problems.

Just getting started? It only takes 10 minutes of exercise to improve your mood according to a study in the July 2001 issue of Health Psychology. If you have not been used to exercise, keep your exercise intensity very low. Then gradually increase tempo and duration as your fitness and mood improves.

12. Increased cognitive function.

Been inactive for 40 plus years? You can still regain mental acuity. Studies at University of Illinois with formerly sedentary 60-75 year olds showed improvement in concentration, planning, and organization. Stimulate your hippocampus with regular exercise. Late life exercising is better than no exercising. It's never too late to start exercising. Studies in Japan showed significant improvement in intelligence tests with 30 minutes of running 2 to 3 times per week. Keep running and you'll maintain your cognitive function better than non-exercisers.

13. Less breast cancer.

Regular exercise decreases breast cancer risk by 20 percent. According to the Archives of Internal Medicine, nurses who exercised more than 7 hours per week had 20 percent less breast cancer than nurses who did less than one hour of vigorous exercise. Sustained walking is sufficient. Walking to your patient and giving patient care is a more active pastime than working at a desk! Walking to your colleague instead of sending an e-mail is fitness enhancing and more sociable. Do some high intensity exercise too and you'll burn more calories.

Exercise decreases all cancer risk, including a 62 percent decrease in upper digestive tract cancer.

14. Exercise reduces Tylenol needs.

Aerobic exercise reduces chronic headaches by reducing stress, by decreasing insomnia, and by increasing your body's secretion of endorphins, which is a natural analgesic. Regular exercisers decrease their Tylenol and other analgesic needs.

15. Problems with Insomnia...exercise is better than a Restoril or other sedative.

Regular aerobic exercise such as walking or running improves the quality of your sleep and decreases the time that it takes to fall asleep. Improving the quality or the duration makes you more productive and happier during your active hours. Exercise at modest intensity for 40 minutes, 2 to 4 hours before you wish to sleep.

16. Exercise for your baby.

Do moderately intensive weight bearing exercise on several days per week during early pregnancy and you'll improve fetoplacental growth rates. Your baby and you will be healthier during and after the birth. Your postpartum recovery will also be faster.

17. Exercise reduces DVTs.

Deep Vein Thrombosis or blood clots kill thousands of Americans every year. Inactivity such as office work and sitting on an airplane increases your DVT risk.

After surgery, early ambulation and gentle range of motion exercises are the key to preventing blood clots in the veins of the large leg muscles, and also decreases the risk of pneumonia. The walking also enhances mood and recovery from the surgery.

Don't wait for a major operation to get your legs moving. Walk a few hundred yards several times a day, and get a 40-minute moderately intensive exercise session most days.

18. Run to increase your libido.

Able to exercise for a couple of hours at a time, with good circulation to your heart and other muscles? You'll have good circulation to your sex glands too. Vigorous exercise increases hormone levels and boosts self-confidence in men and women. Men's testosterone levels rise after a 30 minute run and stay up for 60 minutes! Plan on running with your significant other, even if one of you rides a bike while the other runs.

19. Exercise to beat that Cold.

Exercise makes it easier for you to recover from a cold because your immune cells circulate at a higher rate than when not exercising. However, don't increase your exercise while you have a cold. As stated on page 210, exercise stimulates the production of Human Growth Hormone, which will fight your colds and infections.

INDEX

THE AUTHOR

David Holt, at 31.16 for the 10K and 71 minutes for the half-marathon (2.272 times his 10K time), was never in danger of getting a college scholarship, especially as most of his personal records came after his 30th birthday...the result of over a decade of competent and varied training.

David is a Registered Nurse, who specialized in Orthopedics, and trained with English Cross-country champion and top ten in the World at Cross-country during the 1960s, Gerry North.

At age 45, David cross-trains copiously with biking, elliptical training, pool running, swimming and weight training. Note that they are listed alphabetically!

David Holt's printed books include *Running Dialogue, 10K & 5K Running, Training & Racing, 5K Fitness Run* and *Best Marathons.*

David has sold articles to Runner's World and Running Times. E-books available soon will be:

5K Fitness Run...early races up to the 10K.

Best Marathons: Jog, Run, Train or Walk & Race Fast Marathons.

5K Fitness Walk, Jog or Run for Health: Decrease your death risk from 18 diseases and conditions.

10K & 5K Running: Jog, Run and Train to Race 5K, 10K to 10 Miles (e-book version of the printed 10K & 5K Running)

Athletic Cross Training for Fitness & Life: Pool run, weight or elliptical train, bike & walk or jog to fitness or the Triathlon. Your current Chapters 9 & 10 contains most of this E-book.

401 Injury Prevention and Treatment tips to Walk, Jog, Run or Train 6 days a week.

301 Balanced Eating & Nutrition Tips: Don't Diet for Exercise & Health.

Printed copies of David Holt's books can be ordered from any bookstore (high street or Internet) or direct from the author. Books are $17.95 for the first copy (or $14 per copy if ordering more than one copy). Shipping and sales tax is included. Mail checks or money orders to:
David Holt PO Box 543, Goleta, CA 93116.

Running Dialogue, 5K to the Marathon, 280 pages ISBN # 0965889742 $17.95. An excellent first book for beginners or as an addition to your library for experienced athletes.

10K & 5K Running, Training & Racing: The Running Pyramid, 180 pages ISBN # 0965889718 $17.95. Five training phases for 5K to 10K, from 20 to 100 miles per week. Low intensity 20 mile per week runners enjoy the science and running techniques as much as the 60 or 80 mile per week runners. Each level of runner has a special section.

Best Half Marathons: Jog, Run, Train or Walk & Race the Half Marathon. 216 pages ISBN # 0965889769 $17.95. You have this book!

Best Marathons: Jog, Run, Train or Walk & Race Fast Marathons. 344 pages ISBN # 096588970X $17.95. Five training phases total 10 to 50 weeks to your marathon, plus extensive nutrition and injury avoidance advice.

5K Fitness Run ISBN # 0965889750 168 pages at $14.95 Healthy beginnings to 5K jogging and running at 12 to 30 miles per week, plus extensive cross training advice.

5K Fitness Walk to beat 18 diseases includes nutrition advice, and is $14.95.

The bottom four books are also available as e-books.
David's advice is also at http://www.runningbook.com

P.S. Good running economy or efficiency saves energy and reduces your injury risk.

The author has no doubt that commentators will shriek at the abundance of 15 to 18 miles runs, saying that they are too far merely for half marathon training.

It's rather unfortunate that long runs are the best way to improve your running economy. Once you hit 30 miles per week, it was easy to handle 10 miles at steady pace in one run. However, it's not until you do 14s, 16s and 18s on a regular basis that you learn to significantly:

* Curtail your stride length to reduce jarring and fatigue from overstriding.
* Land close to the rear of your foot;
* Keep your feet close to the ground with minimal knee lift to conserve still more energy;
* With a nice knee bend while your leg is in the support phase;
* Barely move the arms at all while avoiding shoulder roll;
* Yet push off from your calves with a forward motion to propel yourself forward while saving the quadriceps;
* With a slight forward lean;
* Thus making you a smoother runner;
* Long runs teach your muscles to use fatty acids, thus conserving your limited glycogen supply.

Note: Smoother running is also stimulated by sessions of 20 to 30 minutes at anaerobic threshold as covered in Chapter Seven, with hill repeats of one to three minutes up a modest grade as covered in Chapter Three and Interval training (Chapter Eight). However, the long runs of up to 18 miles are the most important element for improving your running economy. The second most important day is when you run 12 miles mid-week! High mileage people also have better running economy, so don't forget those pleasant 5s and 6s between your speed days.